D1050283

SAY IT LIKE
OBAMA
AND WIN!
THE POWER OF SPEAKING
WITH PURPOSE AND VISION

SHEL LEANNE

Expanded Edition

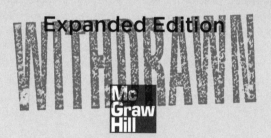

Mc
Graw
Hill

New York Chicago San Francisco Lisbon
London Madrid Mexico City
Milan New Delhi San Juan Seoul
Singapore Sydney Toronto

The McGraw·Hill Companies

1 2 3 4 5 6 7 8 9 0 DOC/DOC 0 1 4 3 2 1 0 9

ISBN 978-0-07-171308-5
MHID 0-07-171308-5

Printed and bound by RR Donnelley.

McGraw-Hill books are available at special quantity discounts to use as premiums and sales promotions, or for use in corporate training programs. For more information, please write to the Director of Special Sales, Professional Publishing, McGraw-Hill, Two Penn Plaza, New York, NY 10121-2298. Or contact your local bookstore.

In most instances, the public remarks of Barack Obama are printed in this book as they were prepared in written form and in some cases, the words Obama actually spoke may vary from the original language. In the cases of Barack Obama's 2004 Democratic Convention keynote address and his 2008 Democratic Convention acceptance speech, which are printed in this book in full, Obama's written remarks have been adjusted to reflect more closely the words he actually spoke aloud where variances occurred.

CONTENTS

CHAPTER 4

WINNING HEARTS AND MINDS

65

CHAPTER 5

CONVEYING VISION

81

CHAPTER 8

FACING AND OVERCOMING CONTROVERSY

155

CHAPTER 9

MOTIVATING OTHERS TO ACTION AND LEAVING STRONG LAST IMPRESSIONS

173

CHAPTER 10

THE SPEECHES THAT
MADE HISTORY

193

ENDNOTES

267

ACKNOWLEDGMENTS

Given the depth of my work in South Africa, I have had the pleasure over the years of meeting some of South Africa's leaders—who are among the world's most esteemed leaders—including Nelson Mandela, Archbishop Desmond Tutu, the late Walter Sisulu, and the late Govan Mbeki. I have greatly benefited from their examples and from our exchanges, and I have since enjoyed sharing the lessons I have learned through my leadership development work. It was an honor to come to understand their vision of the world they hoped to help create. Most of their ideals resembled those I had learned about growing up, when studying in depth about Martin Luther King Jr. Back then, as a young teen, I had enjoyed the privilege of meeting with Coretta Scott King, who had examined one of my early written works and wanted to take the time to encourage me as a writer. Both in the United States and abroad, I have seen that some of the world's greatest leaders have been seeking the same goal—a world in which, as Martin Luther King Jr. put it, people would be judged not "by the color of their skin, but by the content of their character." In light of this background, it was fascinating for me to write this book assessing some of the factors that have helped make President Barack Obama one of the most distinguished leaders and communicators of recent times. It is clear that in many ways, Obama—who transcends race and speaks words of unity—represents what many influential leaders of earlier generations had hoped to see.

I would like here to thank the many people who have supported me over the years. Thank you to my son, Joshua, for being the light of my life. A special thank-you to my parents, Barbara Geiger and the late Dr. David N. Geiger, and my siblings and their spouses: Stacia Geiger-Alston and Thomas Alston, David Geiger, Jr. and Kim Geiger, and Sandra Geiger. Thank you to Christine Baker and Aunt Mildred Geiger, who have provided such mentoring, love, and support. Thank you to my friends and family members who have been particularly faithful with their love during the recent trials of life—including Ted Small, Audrey Gross-Stratford, Yvonne Chang, Ruby Lue Holloway, Reginald Brown, Jane Tanner, David White, Susan Watanabe, and Julie Taylor Vaz.

A hearty thank-you must go also to my aunts and uncles, including William Geiger, Ann Lewis, Edward Geiger, Sr., Joyce and Joe Montgomery, Thomas and Eunice Holloway, Thelma Geiger and family, Sandra and Sam Cook, Andrew Geiger and family, Johnnie Scott and family, and Geraldine Roby and family. Thanks to my wonderful cousins, who include Butch and Tonya Geiger, Derek Geiger, Marty Geiger, Alpha Lavergne, Nat and Veritta Holloway, Pat and Kish Holloway, Carolyn Holloway, Thelma Geiger and family, Jackie Coleman, Yolanda Stevens and family, Luwanda Gandy and family, Andrea Montgomery and family, and the Geigers of Atlanta.

Thank you for the support of Margarita Rodriquez and Cynthia Haines. Thank you to Ochoro Otunnu for his encouragement. A special thanks to my friends Helen-Claire Sievers, Byron Auguste and Emily Bloomfield, the late Ursula Guidry and her family, Laurie Claus, Kweku Ampiah, Paul Rudatsikira, Lorelee Dodge, Andrea Chipman, Julie Catterson, Sister Helen

McCulloch, Carolyn Kramer, and Averill Pritchett. I express my gratitude to the ministers who have fed my mind over the years, including Reverend Dr. H. Beecher Hicks, Jr., Reverend Nolan Williams Jr., and Reverend Raymond Webb and his wife Janet. Thank you to the ministers and members of Irvine Presbyterian Church.

I would like to express my appreciation to my former colleagues at Harvard University and Oxford University, and my current colleagues on the board of WorldTeach, an educational nonprofit. To the Wanyangus, a beautiful Luo family in rural western Kenya: how can I ever thank you for opening your home in rural Kenya to me and sharing your wisdom with me, becoming my "Kenyan family." To the numerous people I continue to work with on HIV/AIDS as I complete a forthcoming book set in Crossroads, South Africa: Thank you! This includes Toby and Aukje Brouwer of Beautiful Gate, who have set such a marvelous example with their lives and work; Khaya Dyantyi of Beautiful Gate, whose tremendous faith in a hopeful tomorrow inspires me; and Dr. Lesley Szabo of Kids with HIV, whose gusto keeps me dreaming of how to keep bringing positive change in the world. Thank you to the many doctors, leaders of HIV support groups, heads of orphanages and HIV support group members I have worked with. You have all greatly enriched my life. I hope my writings and my leadership development work will impact your lives equally well.

Very importantly, a huge thank-you to Mary Glenn for her wonderful guidance, and to Alice Peck for her insights. The support of Peter McCurdy and Tania Loghmani was also greatly appreciated.

INTRODUCTION

"Absolutely masterful. He's a master of the craft."

Those words have described the oratorical strength of Barack Obama, who took the stage at the 2004 Democratic National Convention and electrified America with a rousing keynote address. His twenty-minute speech—less than 2,300 words—captured the imaginations of Americans and garnered praise from around the world. Obama successfully drove his points home, fused the best of rhetoric and substance, focused on a powerful message, and delivered it with great effectiveness. His words and vision inspired millions of viewers. The media instantly dubbed Obama a "Rising Star" and the stirring keynote delivery greatly accelerated the trajectory of his career, transforming him overnight into a distinguished national political figure. Obama went on to successfully build one of the most diverse political movements in American history, shattering historic barriers and becoming the presumptive 2008 Democratic presidential nominee. Few things have helped fuel Obama's rapid political ascension more than his outstanding communication skills.

Say It Like Obama and Win! focuses on the communicative power of Barack Obama and the practices and techniques that have enabled him to take his place as one of the most notable orators of recent times. Obama's political successes underscore a well-established fact: Leaders in all fields benefit when they develop outstanding communication skills, because the ability to convey vision, inspire confidence, persuade, and motivate others is key to effective leadership.

The words used to describe Obama's style—*charismatic, magnetic, energizing*—speak to his strength as a communicator. So, too, do the adjectives invoked to characterize his speeches: *eloquent, inspiring, compelling*. Many observers consider Obama such an accomplished speaker that they compare him with the great communicators of our era—Martin Luther King Jr., John F. Kennedy, Robert Kennedy, Bill Clinton, and Ronald Reagan. Even overseas, Obama's talents and vision have generated excitement. In June 2008, *The Times* reported that Europeans are deeply attracted to Obama's "mixture of Martin Luther King and John F. Kennedy." It observed that, "waves of euphoria swept across the Atlantic . . . after Mr. Obama's victory in the Democratic primary."[1] This enthusiasm was highly evident in July 2008, when Obama attracted an audience of 200,000 for a single speech in Berlin, Germany.

What is Barack Obama doing? What communication practices have enabled him to move rapidly from obscurity, overcoming challenges that could have thwarted another candidate—his race, his youth, his "exotic" name—to become one of the most important figures in the Democratic Party? What oratory skills account for his ability to bring such disparate segments of society together, "transcending" race, energizing millennials (Generation Y voters), and inspiring newcomers—young and old—to participate in the electoral process? How does Obama manage to break down so many barriers? How does he connect so well with listeners, moving them on both an emotional and intellectual level as he translates his vision into the impulse to act? What can leaders in all arenas—business, politics, law, nonprofit and academia—learn from him?

Regardless of what you think of his politics, Obama's achievements since the 2004 Democratic National Convention are striking. Four short years after his keynote address, the first-term junior U.S. Senator who ranked toward the very bottom in Senate seniority went up against the "Clinton machine" in an improbable quest for the Democratic presidential nomination. Obama stepped into a significant place in history when he passed the critical 2118 delegate threshold to become the presumptive Democratic presidential nominee, the first African American major party nominee for U.S. president. It was a historic victory, a watershed moment, one many people believed unthinkable during their lifetimes. Significantly, Obama accepted the Democratic presidential nomination on August 28, 2008, only forty-five years from the very day that Martin Luther King Jr. stood on the Lincoln Memorial and delivered his iconic "I Have a Dream" speech. As the late commentator Tim Russert aptly observed on June 3, 2008: "When you sit and reflect just for a . . . second about what we are witnessing—this young 46-year-old African American man, now the nominee of the Democratic Party. Just put that in the context of our nation and the whole issue of race—it's breathtaking."

Underpinning these notable achievements are Obama's communication abilities. His outstanding oration helped set in motion a so-called phenomenon, with Obama's American rallies attracting audiences as large as 75,000.[2] Observers—noting Obama's accomplishment in expanding the electoral base in an unprecedented manner—called his effort more than a campaign; they deemed it a "movement." With a donor base of nearly 2 million, more individuals are believed to have contributed to Obama's campaign than to any other presidential candidate in American history. In light of Obama's influence and momentum, heavy hitters of the Democratic establishment— Bill Richardson, Edward Kennedy, John Kerry, and John Edwards—were inspired to by-pass long-term loyalties and endorse Obama for president over Hillary Clinton. Given his popularity, Obama even affected popular parlance with newly minted words and phrases: Obama Mamas, Obamacans, Obamacize, Obamanomics, Obamamentum, Obamamania.

Many people credit Obama's astonishing success to his powerful messages of hope that transcend traditional divisions of party, economics, gender, religion, region, and race. Indeed, his speech themes appeal to significant numbers of people. Consider some of the themes: *Change That Works for You, Forging a New Future for America, A More Perfect Union, Keeping America's Promise, Reclaiming the American Dream, Our Moment Is Now, Change We Can Believe In, A New Beginning, Our Common Stake in America's Prosperity, A Sacred Trust, An Honest Government, A Hopeful Future, Take Back America.*

Given the strength of Obama's message, Governor Bill Richardson called Obama's candidacy a "once in a lifetime opportunity for our country" and referred to Obama as "a once in a lifetime leader." Caroline Kennedy concurred in her January 27, 2008 *New York Times* article entitled "A President Like My Father":

Over the years, I've been deeply moved by the people who've told me they wished they could feel inspired and hopeful about America the way people did when my father was president. . . . . All my life, people have told me that my father changed their lives, that they got involved in public service or politics because he asked them to. And the generation he inspired has passed that spirit on to its children. I meet young people who were born long after John F. Kennedy was president, yet who ask me how to live out his ideals.

Sometimes it takes a while to recognize that someone has a special ability to get us to believe in ourselves, to tie that belief to our highest ideals and imagine that together we can do great things. In those rare moments, when such a person comes along, we need to put aside our plans and reach for what we know is possible.

We have that kind of opportunity with Senator Obama.

But there have been other advocates for the middle class and the poor. There have been other leaders with impressive personal stories. There have also been other leaders who have spoken words of unity, goodwill, and hope. What makes Obama so compelling? Why does his message resonate so powerfully? It is more than the message: *it is also how the message is delivered.* This is acknowledged even from across the political aisle. As Louisiana's Republican Governor Bobby Jindal commented on August 10, 2008, "Senator Obama is one of the best speakers— one of the most inspiring speakers—I've seen in a political generation. You have to go back to President Ronald Reagan to really see somebody who's that articulate." Jindal noted that through excellent communication, Obama greatly inspires and motivates people.[3]

The sources of Obama's oratory strength are many. The natural resonance of Obama's deep baritone is an asset. Buttressing this is his impressive ability to control his voice, which he wields like a fine-tuned instrument. He has shown he can alter the texture of his tone to become wistful, indignant, pulsing with optimism and determination—whatever the delivery requires. He has shown skill in quickening his cadence, slowing it down, amplifying the wind beneath his words, and allowing his voice to trail when it suits his needs. He has a keen awareness of when to employ pregnant pauses, metered just right—the intervals long enough to drive points home. He is excellent at creating dynamic images and moving people with effective gestures, sometimes with just one finger. He knows how to draw on an impressive range of rhetoric, and utilizes techniques such as repetition, backward loops, and symbolism to make his pronouncements influence and endure.

Obama knows it isn't enough to form a vision or set goals—success requires an ability to articulate vision and goals in a highly compelling manner. In accounting for Obama's oratorical strength, substance cannot be divorced from style of delivery. *Say It Like Obama and Win!* examines the lessons to be learned from the excellent communication practices that have helped bring about Obama's successes. It illuminates how leaders in all fields—business, politics, law, nonprofit, and academia—can draw from those best practices in order to develop excellent communication abilities.

Chapter 1 presents and annotates the full text of Barack Obama's 2004 Democratic Convention keynote address—the speech that started it all. An examination of this speech reveals many of the key practices Obama employs that give him such distinguished communicative power. Each subsequent chapter delves more deeply into the communication and leadership lessons that we can learn, exploring a variety of Obama's public pronouncements.

Chapter 2, "Earning Trust and Confidence," examines practices that have enabled Obama to inspire and motivate so many people so quickly, winning over many skeptics with his charisma. His success illustrates the importance of a strong first impression and how leveraging an excellent second impression helps foster trust and confidence. We'll look at how his exemplary use of nonverbal language as well as his ability to layer meaning beneath his words work together for striking results.

Chapter 3, "Breaking Down Barriers," explores Obama's exceptional skill in using oration to unify disparate groups. His forthrightness in acknowledging his unconventional background, combined with his skill in projecting this background as "quintessentially American" and his ability to establish common ground, are assets. Reinforcing this, Obama's ability to employ words that resonate has helped him build bridges, drawing out what brings people together rather than what sets them apart.

Chapter 4, "Winning Hearts and Minds," examines the best practices that have helped Barack Obama elicit reactions such as, "His words moved me," and "He understands." His speeches are far from mere recitations—he has demonstrated a remarkable ability to connect with listeners. Key has been his talent for knowing his audiences and identifying the issues they most care about. We'll discuss how he has been able to speak to those issues and how he has succeeded in communicating his empathy and personalizing his messages. What are the techniques behind his style that make the podium and lectern disappear, creating a sense of dinner table talk, as if you are speaking to him one-to-one? We will learn.

Chapter 5, "Conveying Vision," explores practices that have enabled Barack Obama to get his point across so effectively. It studies the lessons to be learned from his skill in using descriptive, multidimensional words, rich with corollary meaning. His ability to humanize ideas, themes and emotions, to employ backward loops and to recount effective anecdotes distinguish him as a speaker, as do the ways he crystallizes his points so that they're remembered long after he has delivered a speech.

Chapter 6, "Driving Points Home," delves into techniques Obama employs to distill his main issues, making them dominant in the listener's mind. Despite significant time constraints—many of his speeches are only twenty minutes long—Obama speaks very effectively, employing an impressive range of rhetorical techniques to convey powerful messages. Among these techniques are conduplicatio, anaphora, epistrophe, mesodiplosis, alliteration, and tricolon. Fancy names, remarkable impact. We show how these techniques allow Obama to home in on key thematic ideas. We also explore how Obama communicates takeaways and slogans with such great effectiveness that many people can recite those slogans with ease.

Chapter 7, "Persuading," explores lessons to be learned about the practices Obama uses to bring others to his way of thinking. When seeking to do more than convey information, but also to impact opinion and encourage action, Obama pays particular attention to emphasizing a strong sense of logic, sequencing ideas, and addressing non-rhetorical questions. Particularly notable is his use of juxtaposition and the antithesis structure as hallmarks of his persuasion style, comparing and contrasting ideas excellently. Together, these techniques help him to elicit a "yes" response—the nod of affirmation of the persuaded listener.

Chapter 8, "Facing and Overcoming Controversy," takes a look at how Barack Obama uses his strong communication skills to weather and survive controversy, often defusing it and mitigating any damaging effects. Whether addressing a poor choice of words or dousing the fire set by the incendiary remarks of Reverend Jeremiah Wright, we see how Obama's communication practices have aided him in efforts to face and overcome controversies. His sincerity, as well as his tendency to address errors head-on and to accept responsibility while standing strong in his beliefs, offer many lessons.

Chapter 9, "Motivating Others to Action and Leaving Strong Last Impressions," explores the communication practices that have helped Obama motivate people to take action. It delves into the tools Obama uses to convey a sense of momentum and build a sense of urgency, while adopting a communication style that makes him seem more accessible to the audience, as if speaking one-to-one. It also explores how Barack Obama's communication style enables him to build to a crescendo, underscoring memorable takeaways and ending strong.

Chapter 10, "The Speeches that Made History," includes historical speeches from Obama's acceptance of the presidential nomination at the Democratic National Convention, the Election Night Victory address, the Inaugural Address, the address to Ghana's Parliament, and the health care reform address to the Joint Session of Congress.

We have much to learn from these practices that, together, have helped make Barack Obama one of the most outstanding communicators of recent times.

CHAPTER 1

THE SPEECH THAT STARTED IT ALL

On a night of the 2004 Democratic National Convention, Barack Obama stepped onstage and electrified America with his keynote address. His discourse, widely hailed as inspiring and eloquent, provides a valuable snapshot of the excellent communication practices Obama employs as he harnesses the power of speaking with purpose and vision. Through his delivery, we learn how substance and style can work together to increase the effectiveness and impact of communication.

This chapter presents the 2004 keynote address in full. Obama's written words are annotated with references to some of the gestures, tone, and pacing techniques he employed in delivering his career-accelerating address. Let's look at what made the 2004 speech such a success.

⤐ 2004 DEMOCRATIC NATIONAL CONVENTION ⤏
KEYNOTE ADDRESS, JULY 27, 2004

In the minutes before Barack Obama takes to the stage, Illinois Senator Dick Durbin sings Obama's praises to the Boston audience and to millions of TV viewers. He refers to Barack Obama as a man whose "life celebrates the opportunity of America . . . family reflects the hope of an embracing nation . . . values rekindle our faith in a new generation. . . ." He praises Obama for having "the extraordinary gift to bring people together of all different backgrounds."

Barack Obama walks onto the stage with a brisk, purposeful, confident gait. He makes immediate visual contact with the audience, clapping his hands along with them—the first signs of connection. He stretches his arm toward the audience in an open-palmed wave and then greets Durbin with a warm embrace that signifies the deep respect of dear friends. With applause still ringing, Obama makes his way to the lectern, planting his feet firmly, shoulders squared. He touches each hand to the lectern, possessing it—a posture of confidence and authority. With chin lifted, he bows ever-so-slightly to the audience, his gesture of appreciation and gratitude. As the applause continues, Obama folds his hands neatly on the lectern and smiles humbly, seeming to gain strength from the crowd's enthusiasm.

As the applause subsides, Obama thanks Senator Durbin. He takes in a breath and the resonant baritone of his voice rolls as he begins his 2004 Democratic National Convention keynote address:

On behalf of the great state of Illinois, [*the crowd applauds, and Obama's eyes sparkle with pride at speaking the name of his home state*] crossroads of a nation [*pause*], Land of Lincoln, let me express my deepest gratitude for the privilege of addressing this convention. [*He reaches out to the audience with open hands, conveying his gratitude.*]

Tonight is a particular honor for me because, let's face it, my presence on this stage is pretty unlikely. [*Obama places his hand over his heart. His intonation underscores the irony of the circumstances.*] My father was a foreign student, born and raised in a small village in Kenya. He grew up herding goats, went to school in a tin-roof shack. His father, my grandfather, was a cook, a domestic servant to the British. [*He pinches the fingers of his right hand, underscoring his point.*]

But my grandfather had larger dreams for his son. [*Obama stretches his palms upwards, as if measuring the enormity of the dreams.*] Through hard work and perseverance my father got a scholarship to study in a *magical* place: *America* [*italics added for emphasis*], that shone as a beacon of freedom and opportunity to so many who had come before. [*His inflection conveys patriotic pride and generates applause.*]

While studying here, my father met my mother. She was born in a town on the other side of the world, in Kansas. [*Obama gestures with a hand off in a direction, indicating far, far away. He flashes a bright smile toward the part of the crowd that cheers upon hearing "Kansas" and waves to them in a tender gesture.*] Her father worked on oil rigs and farms through most of the Depression. The day after Pearl Harbor my grandfather signed up for duty, joined Patton's army, marched across Europe. Back home, my grandmother raised a baby *and* [*emphasis*] went to work on a bomber assembly line. After the war, they studied on the GI Bill, bought a house through FHA, and later moved west, all the way to Hawaii, in search of opportunity.

And they, too, had big dreams for their daughter, a common dream, born of two continents. My parents shared not only an improbable love; they shared an *abiding* faith in the possibilities of this nation. [*Obama speaks the words with pride and reverence; his hand extended to the audience, signifying shared awe in all the United States has to give.*]

They would give me an African name, Barack, or "blessed," [*he touches his hand over his heart*] believing that in a *tolerant* [*emphasis*] America [*he pinches the fingers of his right hand*] your name is no barrier to success. [*Applause.*] They *imagined* me going to the best schools in the land, *even though they weren't rich*, because in a *generous* America you don't have to be rich [*he raises a palm to the crowd, a little stop sign, as if to halt any notion that richness is a precursor to success*] to achieve your potential. [*Applause.*] They are both passed away now. Yet, I know that, on this night, they look down on me with great pride.

I stand here today, grateful for the diversity of my heritage, aware that my parents' dreams live on in my two precious daughters. [*Sincerity rings in his tone.*] I stand here knowing that my story is part of the larger American story [*he stretches a hand to the audience, reaching out to them*], that I owe a debt to all of those who came before me, and that, in no other country on earth is my story even possible. [*He pinches his fingers with those words, his voice bursting with pride. He pauses as some audience members rise in ovation.*]

Tonight, we gather to affirm the greatness of our nation, not because of the height of our skyscrapers, or the power of our military, or the size of our economy. Our pride is based on a very simple premise, summed up in a declaration made over two hundred years ago, "We hold these truths to be self-evident, [*he amplifies his voice slightly, speaking the patriotic words with care and curls his right fingers into a C, motioning in front of him as if setting the words on air*] that all men are created equal. [*Applause.*] That they are endowed by their Creator with certain inalienable rights. That among these are life, liberty, and the pursuit of happiness."

That [*emphasis*] is the true genius of America [*applause*], a faith in simple dreams, an insistence on small miracles. That we can tuck in our children at night and know they are fed and clothed and safe from harm. That we can say what we think, write what we think, without hearing a sudden knock on the door. [*Obama knocks a balled fist on an imaginary door.*] That we can have an idea and start our own business without paying a bribe. That we can participate in the political process without fear of retribution, and that our votes will be counted—at least, most of the time. [*He allows his tone to fall flat, disapproving, signaling a wry reference to the disputed 2000 U.S. presidential election results. The audience responds with jeers, sharing his disapproval.*]

This year, in this election, we are called to reaffirm our values and our commitments, to hold them against a hard reality, and see how we are measuring up to the legacy of our forbearers, and the promise of future generations. And fellow Americans—Democrats, Republicans, Independents—I say to you tonight: we have more work to do. [*Obama stresses the words, his tone issuing the statement as a challenge. More applause.*] More work to do for the workers I met in Galesburg, Illinois, who are losing their union jobs at the Maytag plant that's moving to Mexico, and now are having to compete with their own children for jobs that pay seven bucks an hour. [*His tone rings with disapproval.*] More to do for the father that I met who was losing his job and choking back the tears, wondering how he would pay $4,500 a month for the drugs his son needs without the health benefits that he counted on. [*His tone conveys great empathy.*] More to do for the young woman in East St. Louis, and thousands more like her, who *has the grades, has the drive, has the will* [*he emphasizes the words and his slight pauses add power to the delivery*], but doesn't have the money to go to college.

Now, don't get me wrong. The people I meet in small towns and big cities, in diners and office parks, they don't expect government to solve all their problems. They know they have to work hard to get ahead, and *they want to.* [*Obama stresses the words as he pinches his fingers to further accentuate his statement.*] Go into the collar counties around Chicago, and people will tell you they don't want their tax money wasted by a welfare agency *or by the Pentagon.* [*His amplification of these last four words makes a negative reference to the Iraq War, drawing reaction from the audience.*] Go into any inner city neighborhood, and folks will tell you that government alone can't teach our kids to learn. They know that parents have to teach, that children can't achieve unless we raise their expectations [*he gestures upward as if raising a bar*], and turn off the television sets and eradicate the slander that says a black youth with a book is acting white. [*He wags his index finger, as if chastising someone for that belief.*] They know those things. [*Enthusiastic applause.*] People don't expect government to solve all their problems. [*He lifts a vertical palm to the audience, as if halting the very notion.*] But they sense, *deep in their bones* [*he raises a soft fist and thumps it in air*], that with just a slight change in priorities [*he moves his right fingers as if turning a knob slightly to adjust it*], we can make sure that every child in America has a decent shot at life, and that the doors of opportunity remain open to all. *They know,* [*he pinches his fingers, underscoring his emphasis of the words*] we can do better [*a brief pause*], and they want that choice.

In this election, [*Obama raises his index finger in the air, raising it like a staff*] we offer that choice. Our party has chosen a man to lead us who embodies the best this country has to offer. [*Pride rings in his tone.*] And that man is John Kerry. [*His tone is firm and resolute. Applause.*] John Kerry understands the ideals of community, faith, and service, because they've defined his life. [*He pinches his fingers to give each word weight.*] From his heroic service in Vietnam to his years as prosecutor and lieutenant governor, through two decades in the United States Senate, he has devoted himself to this country. [*He turns both palms upward, as if presenting a gift or offering, underscoring his description of Kerry's devotion and service.*] Again and again, we've seen him make tough choices when easier ones were available. His values and his record affirm what is best in us. [*He varies his tone and amplifies his volume.*]

John Kerry believes in an America where hard work is rewarded. So instead of offering tax breaks to companies shipping jobs overseas [*Obama motions his hand off dismissively to the right*], he offers them to companies creating jobs here at home. [*He moves both hands to the left as if moving an object to where it belongs, signifying how much more Kerry would give to the alternative of keeping jobs at home. Applause.*]

John Kerry believes in an America where *all* [*emphasis*] Americans can afford the same health coverage our politicians in Washington have for themselves. [*Applause.*] John Kerry believes in energy independence, so we aren't held hostage to the profits of oil companies [*Obama motions his hand like a stop sign*] or the sabotage of foreign oil fields. [*Applause.*] John Kerry believes in the constitutional freedoms that have made our country the envy of the world, and he will never sacrifice our basic liberties nor use faith as a wedge to divide us. [*Pause for applause.*] And John Kerry believes that in a dangerous world, war must be an option sometimes [*he points his index finger in the air, signifying the importance*], but it should never be the *first* [*emphasis*] option. [*Applause.*]

A while back, I met a young man named Shamus in a VFW Hall in East Moline, Illinois. He was a good-looking kid, six-two, six-three, clear-eyed, with an easy smile [*the texture of Obama's tone is wistful, conveying admiration*]. He told me he'd joined the marines and was heading to Iraq the following week. As I listened to him explain why he'd enlisted, the absolute faith he had in our country and its leaders, his devotion to duty and service, I thought this young man was all that any of us might ever hope for in a child [*he speaks the words with tender affection*]. But then I asked myself: Are we serving Shamus as well as he's serving us? I thought of the 900 men and women, sons and daughters, husbands and wives, friends and neighbors, who won't be returning to their own hometowns. I thought of families I had met who were struggling to get by without a loved one's full income, or whose loved ones had returned with a limb missing or nerves shattered, but still lacked long-term health benefits because they were reservists. [*Disappointment rings in his voice. Applause.*] When we send our young men and women into harm's way, we have a solemn obligation [*he rests his palm over his heart*] not to fudge the numbers [*he raises his hand in a stop sign*], or shade the truth about why they're going, to care for their families while they're gone [*he points an index finger, emphasizing the importance*], to tend to the soldiers upon their return, and to *never* [*pause*] *ever* [*he amplifies his voice greatly*] go to war without enough troops to *win* the war, *secure* the peace, and *earn the respect of the world.* [*He stresses the words, amplifying each to build to a high. Audience members rise in ovation.*]

Now let me be clear. [*Obama motions his index finger up in the air.*] We have real enemies in the world. These enemies must be *found.* [*He pinches his fingers. A slight pause gives gravity to the words.*] They must be *pursued* [*his hand gesture underscores the importance of "pursuing"*], and they must be *defeated.* [*He pinches his fingers at these words, high-*

lighting their importance.] John Kerry knows this. And just as *Lieutenant* [*emphasis*] Kerry did not hesitate to risk his life to protect the men who served with him in Vietnam, *President* [*emphasis*] Kerry will not hesitate *one moment* [*emphasis*] to use our military might to keep America safe and secure. John Kerry *believes* [*emphasis*] in America. And he knows that it's not enough for just some of us to prosper. [*He moves his index finger in the air.*] For alongside our famous individualism, there's another ingredient in the American saga. [*His tone conveys a challenge beneath his words.*]

A belief that we're all connected as one people. [*His tone is filled with wistful, patriotic pride.*] If there's a child on the south side of Chicago who can't read, that *matters to me* [*he moves his hand to his chest, stressing the heartfelt words*], even if it's not my child. [*Obama speaks the words with sincerity and evokes applause.*] If there's a senior citizen somewhere who can't pay for their prescription drug and has to choose between medicine and the rent, that makes my life poorer, even if it's not my grandparent. [*He places his hand tenderly over his heart and draws more applause.*] If there's an Arab American family being rounded up without benefit of an attorney or due process [*he amplifies his tone*], that threatens *my* [*emphasis*] civil liberties. [*He taps a closed fist at his chest, drawing loud cheers from the audience. He pauses as applause rings on.*] It is that fundamental belief—*I am my brother's keeper* [*he raises his volume even more, and his voice rings with moral rightness as he slices a hand through the air*], *I am my sister's keeper* [*he cuts his hand through the air again, making eye contact with the other side of the audience*]—that makes this country work. [*Applause.*] It's what allows us to pursue our individual dreams, and yet still come together as one American family [*his tone grows reflective.*] "E pluribus unum." [*He enunciates each word carefully, curls his right fingers into a C and motions as if placing the words on air for the audience to see, and gives a dramatic pause.*] Out of many, one. [*He lowers his pitch to emphasize the translation and curls his left fingers into a C, motioning again as if placing the words on air.*]

Now, even as we speak, there are those who are preparing to divide us, the spin masters, the negative ad peddlers who embrace the politics of anything goes. Well, I say to them tonight, there is not a *liberal* [*emphasis*] America and a *conservative* America [*he amplifies his volume, his tone mocking the notions*]—there is the *United States of America.* [*Obama enunciates each word carefully—U-ni-ted-States-of-A-mer-i-ca—moving his fingers as if writing in cursive. Applause.*] There is not a *black America* [*emphasis*] and *white America* [*emphasis*] and Latino America and Asian America; there's the *United States of America.* [*He enunciates the words carefully again, giving them dramatic impact. Applause.*] The pundits like to slice and dice our country into red states and blue states. [*His tone mocks the practice.*] Red states for Republicans, blue states for Democrats. But I've got news for them, too. [*He raises his index finger, chastising the pundits.*] We worship an *awesome* God [*he stresses the words, raising his hands and amplifying his voice to signify God's greatness*] in the blue states, and we don't like federal agents poking around in our libraries in the red states. [*He increases his cadence dramatically, underscoring the point.*

Applause.] We coach Little League in the blue states and yes we've got some gay friends in the red states. [*Applause.*] There are patriots who opposed the war in Iraq and there are patriots who supported the war in Iraq. We are *one* [*emphasis*] people, *all of us* [*emphasis*] pledging allegiance to the stars and stripes, *all of us* [*emphasis*] defending the [*pause*] *United States of America.* [*He punches the words—U-ni-ted-States-of-A-mer-i-ca—scrawling his fingers as if writing in cursive. Applause. The electrified audience starts chanting "Obama! Obama!"*]

In the end, that's what this election is about. Do we participate in a politics of cynicism [*his voice falls flat, signaling disapproval*] or do we participate in a politics of hope? [*Obama raises his pitch, sounding hopeful and expectant. The crowd shouts out, "Hope!" as if participating in a "call and response."*] John Kerry calls on us to hope. John Edwards calls on us to hope. I'm not talking about blind optimism here—the almost willful ignorance that thinks unemployment will go away if we just don't think about it, or the health care crisis will solve itself if we just ignore it. That's not what I'm talking about. I'm talking about something *more substantial.* [*Emphasis.*] It's *the hope* [*emphasis*] of slaves sitting around a fire singing freedom songs; *the hope* [*emphasis*] of immigrants setting out for distant shores; *the hope* [*emphasis*] of a young naval lieutenant bravely patrolling the Mekong Delta; *the hope* [*emphasis*] of a mill worker's son who dares to defy the odds; *the hope* [*emphasis*] of a *skinny kid* [*emphasis*] with a funny name [*he thumps his palm against his chest, indicating he is speaking of himself*] who believes that America has a place for him, too. [*He* reaches open palms toward his listeners. The audience goes wild with adulation, the applause extending so long that Obama adds two sentences as the cheers continue.] Hope [emphasis] in the face of difficulty. [His amplified words signify his approval of the audience's reaction.] Hope in the face of uncertainty. [He keeps his volume powerful.] The audacity of hope! [His volume rises.]

In the end, that is God's greatest gift to us, the bedrock [emphasis] of this nation; a belief [emphasis] in things not seen; a belief [emphasis] that there are better days ahead. [Passion resonates in Obama's voice.] I believe [emphasis] that we can give our middle class relief and provide working families with a road to opportunity. I believe [emphasis] we can provide jobs to the jobless, homes to the homeless, and reclaim young people in cities across America from violence and despair. I believe [emphasis] that we have a righteous wind in our backs and that as we stand on the crossroads of history, we can make the right choices, and meet the challenges that face us. America! [emphasis] Tonight! [The intensity of his tone rings like a challenge, reaching a crescendo.]

If you feel the same energy [emphasis] that I do, if you feel the same urgency [emphasis] that I do, if you feel the same passion [emphasis] that I do, if you feel the same hopefulness [emphasis] that I do—if we do what we must do, then I have no doubt that all across the country, from Florida to Oregon [he slices a hand through the air], from Washington to Maine [he slices a hand through air again, his inflections rising and falling to convey the breadth of the geography, from coast to coast] the people will rise up in November, and John

Kerry will be sworn in as president, and John Edwards will be sworn in as vice president, and this country will reclaim its promise, and out of this long political darkness a brighter day will come.

Thank you very much everybody. [*He stretches his arm high, waving good-bye*] God bless you. [*The energized audience rises in full ovation, with some people chanting "Obama! Obama!"*] [Emphases provided.]

In this 2004 keynote address, we see many of the outstanding communication practices that have helped make Barack Obama one of the most compelling speakers of our time. Public and media praise for Obama's keynote address was immediate. "One of the best [addresses] we've heard in many, many years. . . . He's a rising star," Wolf Blitzer declared. "That's as good as they come. . . . This is a fellow who is talking beyond the Democratic base to the whole country. . . . It was terrific," political analyst Jeff Greenfield commented. In the days to come, the press continued to commend the address as a masterpiece of oration. Many of the outstanding communication techniques Obama employed during his keynote address are worth highlighting here.

⇥ EFFECTIVE USE OF BODY LANGUAGE ⇤ AND VOICE

In the delivery of his 2004 keynote address, Barack Obama demonstrated outstanding use of body language. His confident gait, squared shoulders, and commanding stance reached out to the audience, set the tone, and opened a positive dialogue with the viewing public. In short, Obama created a very strong first impression. The deep timbre of his voice, his natural asset, heightened the positive impression. The way he controlled his voice—amplifying it when appropriate, gliding up a half-octave when needed, or allowing it to fall flat to denote disapproval—gave power to his words and helped highlight his key themes. Varying the emotional texture of his tone—making it wistful at times, affectionate at others, and indignant when appropriate—also gave great depth to his words.

Obama's gestures were equally effective—knocking on an imaginary door with a balled fist, pinching his fingers, placing imaginary words on air, holding his palm like a stop sign. They all combined to drive points home. Similarly, placing his hand over his heart at key moments conveyed the sincerity of his words. Obama came across as authentic. His gestures served as masterful elements of delivery.

⇥ ESTABLISHING COMMON GROUND ⇤

In the keynote address, we also see how Barack Obama addressed the "elephant in the room"—his unconventional background, which he skillfully projected as a quintessentially American story of immigration, hard work, and the American Dream. Obama wove in references to his family and Pearl Harbor, Patton's army, a U.S. bomber assembly line, the GI Bill, and FHA mortgage funding, thereby connecting himself to historic "apple pie" American experiences. The mention of these American hallmarks became his credentials for asserting that, in spite of his "exotic" name, he was just like every American. Obama placed himself squarely in the progression of history, demonstrating that he was dreaming the same dreams as most Americans.

Obama's choice of words also helped establish common ground. *Generous America. Beacon of freedom and opportunity. Faith in the possibilities of this nation.* This language resonated with the audience, tapping into patriotic sentiment. In a masterful way, Obama also wove in references to bible verses: *Belief in things not seen . . . I am my brother's keeper. . . . I am my sister's keeper. . . .* He lauded these references as "simple truth." The biblical words and principles reached across divisions of race, class, and party, helping him connect with the audience. Simultaneously, Obama demonstrated his talents as he effortlessly transitioned from discussing biblical truths and linking them to America, to relating these truths to what *he* believes, creating the sense of a strong continuum. With these techniques, Obama successfully broke down barriers and built bridges.

SPEAKING TO AUDIENCE CONCERNS: WINNING HEARTS AND MINDS

Obama demonstrated his ability to tap into the prevailing mood, strengthening the impact of his words by providing details and personalizing his message. When he spoke about the prevailing mood of many Americans who were tired of old-style politicking, he said, "There's not a liberal America and a conservative America. There's a United States of America." Like leaders such as John F. Kennedy, Obama made a meaningful connection with his audience.

As Obama offered specific examples about Americans facing challenges—like a father who had lost his job and needed to pay for his son's medicine—he connected with the audience, demonstrating that he understood intimately the concerns of middle

America and could relate to these challenges. Similarly, as he personalized his message, explaining his deeply held belief in helping the middle class and working families, he won people over by speaking to them directly, almost intimately, and illustrating that their concerns were his concerns too.

⇥ CONVEYING VISION THROUGH PERSONALIZATION ⇤ AND WORDS THAT RESONATE

In his keynote address, Obama employed a wide range of techniques to convey his vision. Vivid language, symbolic words, and personalized ideas were among his tools. His language painted pictures in the minds of listeners: *Slice and dicing us . . . We are one people, all of us pledging allegiance to the Stars and Stripes.* He tied the notion of hope to the experiences of slaves and immigrants and personalized the issue of the Iraq War through references to one particular soldier—Shamus—whose "easy smile" we could visualize instantly. These all provided rich, multilayered communication, conveying vision and ideas excellently.

⇥ DRIVING POINTS HOME ⇤

Obama also employed an effective range of rhetorical techniques as he drove his central points home. Repetition was a primary tool. His repeated references to hope, with carefully constructed sentence structures, underscored the theme. Similarly, stating "John Kerry believes" five times in six sentences reinforced the image of Kerry that Obama sought to stress. Obama's skillful use of repetition focused attention on key themes, making them more memorable.

⇥ EXCELLENT PERSUASION TECHNIQUES ⇤

In the 2004 keynote address, we also saw one of Obama's hall-mark practices for persuasion: the use of juxtaposition for comparison and contrast. For instance, juxtaposition helped him crystallize the importance of the country's founding principles:

> Tonight, we gather to affirm the greatness of our nation, not because of the height of our skyscrapers, or the power of our military, or the size of our economy. Our pride is based on a very simple premise, summed up in a declaration made over two hundred years ago, "We hold these truths to he self-evident, that all men are created equal. That they are endowed by their Creator with certain inalienable rights. That among these are life, liberty and the pursuit of happiness."

His use of juxtaposition also crystallized the argument that Americans are one people and should move forward with unity: "There's not a *liberal* America and a *conservative* America—there's the *United States of America*."

⇥ BUILDING TO A CRESCENDO AND LEAVING ⇤ A STRONG LAST IMPRESSION

Finally, few people can forget the outstanding ending to the moving 2004 keynote address. Obama skillfully varied the rhythm of his words, emphasizing words at key times and amplifying his voice progressively as he built toward a crescendo. He knew how to ride the wave of applause so as not to stall momentum. Once he reached his high point, he ended his address passionately, issuing a challenge, a call to action: "Tonight! If you feel the *same energy* that I do, if you feel the *same urgency* that I do, if you feel the *same passion* that I do, if you feel the *same hopefulness* that I do—if we do what we must do, then . . ."

This powerful ending further energized the audience, leaving them a strong last impression.

Together, these highly effective communication practices enabled Obama to deliver a masterful speech that greatly accelerated the trajectory of his political career and transformed him into an influential national political figure. Now, let's delve further into these practices that have made Barack Obama one of the most distinguished orators of recent times.

CHAPTER 2

EARNING TRUST AND CONFIDENCE

If you aspire to be a highly effective leader, people must trust your judgment and ethics and have confidence in your leadership abilities, believing that you are worthy of authority. In the absence of trust and confidence, nothing else follows. A first task of every aspiring leader, therefore, is to earn the trust and confidence of those they seek to lead. Barack Obama has done this with great success, gaining the trust and confidence of the broad array of people who make up his diverse coalition—everyday citizens, politicians, large donors, policymakers, members of the media establishment. He has drawn on this trust and confidence to capture key opportunities and expand his influence. Key communication practices have aided Obama in his quest. Using communication as a tool for gaining support, Obama has displayed great personal charisma. He takes steps to form a strong first impression and to leverage excellent second impressions. Obama also employs effective gestures, skillfully uses props, gets off to strong beginnings, and conveys admirable ethics. This chapter explores these practices, which have enabled Barack Obama to earn the trust and confidence of millions of supporters both at home and abroad.

⇥ CHARISMA OF A LEADER ⇤

Most people say they know charisma when they see it—that certain fire in the eyes, passion, and command. They point, for example, to political leaders such as Martin Luther King Jr., Ronald Reagan, John F. Kennedy, and Bhenazir Bhutto, and to popular leaders such as Oprah Winfrey. Dynamic leaders. Not the sort to give humdrum, droning speeches; far from the listless speaker who is unenthusiastic about their topic.

The words often invoked to describe Barack Obama—magnetic, electrifying, energizing, and inspiring—speak of his charisma as a leader. Obama has a presentation and style that enable him to earn the confidence of listeners, inspire them, and move them to action. Obama manages to captivate audiences. From the moment he steps in front of an audience with his confident gait, people see a blend of passion and authority. He conveys charisma through many nonverbal attributes—the bright, broad smile; the confident sparkle in the eyes; his resonant voice; and body movement suggesting authority. Part of Obama's charisma involves his ability to convey his enthusiasm and passion effectively. He usually appears closely wedded to the things he talks about, cares deeply about the subjects, and is eager to share. His enthusiasm energizes people young and old.

Perhaps as important as having charisma is the ability to use it to establish an excellent first impression. First impressions last. This well-worn saying is true. In rising as fast as he has, from obscurity to winning the 2008 presidential election, Barack Obama has developed a formidable ability to establish a great first impression.

⇥ CREATING STRONG FIRST IMPRESSIONS— ⇤ IMAGE AND BODY LANGUAGE

A first impression is a critically defining moment. The instant one person first moves into the presence of another, an opinion is formed. Even before you utter any words, you open a dialogue and have spoken volumes through image and body language. The strong first impression that Barack Obama makes reminds us that body movement and image speak a language to the audience as potent as anything said out loud.

Indeed, a highly influential executive coach and author of the book, *CEO Material,* D.A. Benton, once asked a group of young leaders at McKinsey & Company to imagine what they would do if they wanted to make people around them believe they were blind, even though they were not. She prodded them to consider how they would try to look and act. Perhaps they would wear a pair of dark glasses, get a white cane and use that cane to feel their way across the floor. They might walk slowly or haltingly, displaying a bit of uncertainty about the path ahead. They might even get a guide dog and allow it to steer them down the street. In short, they would dress the part, act the part, and gather the right props. She then asked the group to consider the implications if they were seeking instead to project themselves as leaders.

The exercise was useful. Persons seeking to present themselves as leaders should dress the part, act the part, and gather the right props around them. This is because—without uttering a word—through first impressions these actions begin a dialogue and can lay an important foundation for commanding authority, gaining trust, and exercising effective leadership.

Barack Obama is adept at establishing excellent first impressions. The purposeful walk. The visual contact he makes with audiences early on, stretching his arm to them in a confident wave, narrowing the physical distance between himself and the audience. These mark the beginnings of a two-way conversation of sorts—it elicits a sit-up-and-listen response from audience members.

Good eye contact has also been valuable to Obama. Like Bill Clinton, he is perceived as never hesitating to establish firm eye contact; he thrives on connecting with members of his audience and is energized, not drained, by them. As Obama talks, he looks to one side of the room, sometimes with a slight nod of acknowledgment in that direction, and then to the other side. He varies his gaze throughout his discussions; by doing so naturally and smoothly, he pulls listeners in to his talks and engages audience members more fully. Audiences perceive this as respectful—the behavior of a person welcoming them. They also interpret the actions as trustworthy—the behavior of a person willing to look them in the eyes. Those good first impressions last.

The confidence displayed by Obama's pat-on-the-back greetings with some people who introduce him is also an early action that communicates his comfort. He is at ease. Standing before audiences, feet placed firmly and shoulders squared—the message is one of confidence and authority. Where there is a lectern, he often places his hands on each side of it, taking control. The lectern is clearly not a crutch, nor does Obama allow it to serve as an obstacle between him and the audience.

Imagine if, instead of displaying such confidence, Obama had walked onto the 2004 convention stage with his chin lowered, his gait hesitant, and he had offered only a sheepish wave. What a vastly different image that would have conveyed. By contrast, leaders who walk with a purposeful gait, stretch their arm and wave confidently establish a more commanding image and expand their presence. It is best to get off to a strong start and avoid situations in which you must work hard to reverse the damage of a poor first impression. Outstanding communicators take care to use image and body language in ways that wield a highly positive impact.

⇥ LEVERAGING SECOND IMPRESSIONS— ⇤ VOICE AND INTONATION

Another important means of earning trust and confidence can be seen through effective use of voice and intonation. After a leader comes out with a commanding, confident air, exuding the charisma of a leader, then what? Voice and intonation play a role here; both are important tools for increasing the effectiveness of communication.

Voice

One dimension of voice that creates an immediate impression is the *quality* of the voice—its natural pitch and resonance. For Barack Obama, his commanding baritone is a natural asset. It sounds pleasing to the ears and is very authoritative. For most speakers, natural tone quality can be improved and enhanced with practice and voice techniques.

Beyond natural tone quality, the precise way leaders use their voices becomes important to the impressions formed and how effective a speech ultimately is. There are multiple dimensions of the verbal communication beyond the words actually spoken. *How* the words are said can transform a bland recitation into a powerful speech. The tools of the skillful speaker include volume, voice texture, pitch, pace, and inflection. Effective voice and intonation can move people, make words more memorable, and make the communication more effective overall. Talks, delivered powerfully, can elicit responses such as, "Something tugged inside of me." Barack Obama achieves this sort of impact through skillful use of his voice and intonation, which reinforces the substance of his messages.

Amplification

Barack Obama has shown the power of amplifying the voice at key moments. He uses volume to increase excitement as an audience rallies to his opinions. He knows how to stress important words at the right times, giving them an emphatic feel. He increases his volume when reaching a crescendo, the point when he hits the climax of his talk and underscores a key message. Just as he puts power in his volume when rousing a crowd, he knows how to allow his voice to trail off when speaking of something of which he disapproves. Amplifying and washing away—Barack Obama uses volume to enhance the efficacy of his delivery.

Pacing and Pregnant Pauses

Obama's outstanding use of pacing also greatly enhances the effectiveness of his communication. With well-chosen pacing, he slows when enunciating important ideas he wants to settle into the psyches of the listeners. He adopts clipped sentences at the right times, which helps to drive points home. The increase and decrease of his cadence allows him to draw listeners' attention to his most significant points.

Obama is also adept at leveraging silence and employing pregnant pauses. With pregnant pauses, Obama focuses attention on his more important themes, making his remarks more notable. He is also skilled at knowing when to let the silence endure a bit—very dramatic pauses that often elicit reaction from the audience.

Pitch and Emotional Texture

When assessing what makes Barack Obama such a powerful orator, it is easy to observe that he avoids drab recitations. He skillfully employs his delivery techniques. He has made an art of varying his volume and vocal color. The range of the inflections he uses—changes in the pitch of his voice—is also one of his strengths. He varies how he vocalizes key words, drawing on a range of vocal pitch to deepen the impact of what he says in a manner that cannot be achieved by the written word alone. His voice rises and falls when needed. For example, Obama knows how to drop his pitch, pulling on his lower register, and slow his cadence when he wishes to focus on a point, like underlining key words on a chalkboard.

Obama is also a master of strengthening his communication with vocal color. He can make his voice wistful, hopeful, dismissive, and a host of other emotional textures, as circumstances require. His ability to alter the emotional texture of his voice, which he reinforces with effective gestures, increases the impact of his communication.

Taken together, voice and intonation—emphasizing words at the right time, quickening or slowing the cadence, varying the tonal color, varying the rhythm of words—can result in superior communication power. Speeches and remarks become dynamic and full of impact and thereby part of a successful leader's strategic tool set.

⇥ USING EFFECTIVE GESTURES ⇤

Obama breaks the rule suggesting that gestures should be used sparingly. Frequent gesturing is part of his communication style. This works well for him because the movements are fluid and extensions of his words, and they convey his enthusiasm. They work in tandem with modulations of his voice and tone, and they thereby animate his words, providing valuable dimension to his remarks.

Obama's power as an orator helps illustrate that gestures can improve the impact of communication in multiple ways. For one, when used well, gestures create an impression that a speaker is at ease and relating well with the audience. Barack Obama, in particular, employs gestures in ways that create the feel of a one-to-one conversation, as if he is standing next to you conversing, rather than standing on a podium addressing an audience. His gestures help narrow the distance. Whether this involves an outstretched hand to the audience, pinched fingers at appropriate times, or a raised hand, his gestures transform his speeches into dialogues and establish a sense that you are standing near him enjoying an animated conversation.

The use of gestures can also create the sense that a speaker is deeply invested in a topic and earnest in their desire to get others to see their points. For example, a hand placed sincerely over the heart shows deeply felt emotion. Additionally, effective gestures make speech more lively, engaging, and memorable. Cupping fingers in a C, as if placing words on air. Waving an index finger side-to-side, chastising. Motioning fingers toward oneself, beckoning someone near. A "disdainful flick" of the hand, shooing someone away. A soft fist. A closed fist. A palm held out to the audience in a little stop sign. These and countless other gestures can breathe life into speech. As Obama has shown, the precision of certain gestures enhances the descriptive content of oration and underscores key ideas, increasing the potency of spoken words.

⇥ MAXIMIZING PROPS ⇤

The use of props can be another important way to create impressions as well as to reinforce key messages. Consider our earlier example: if you want to convince others you are blind, what props would you use? Sunglasses, a dog, a white cane? Now extend the example. If political candidates are attempting to look presidential, what props might they use? They might flank themselves with large national flags on each side of a lectern. If speakers are trying to look strong on foreign policy, what props might they use? They might choose to invite military leaders to stand behind them when they make their foreign policy pronouncements.

If a speaker is seeking to present themselves as a leader, what props are appropriate? While the answers will depend in part upon the circumstances—the type of audience and its mood, or the subject and goal of the talk, for instance—the role of props in creating impressions should not be overlooked. For the Democrat seeking to connect with Republicans, a red tie conveys a subtle message. For leaders seeking to demonstrate their religious values, they might choose to deliver a speech in a church, where the physical background frames their comments. Similarly, leaders seeking to project authority in a casual setting might choose to forgo the coat and tie, dressing only a tad bit more formally than the audience. They might also arrange the room in a way that will make the audience comfortable (perhaps a room with chairs formed in a circle and no podium, rather than a more formal setting of a podium and lectern). Props—what others call staging—are an important source of nonverbal messaging. Carefully choosing backgrounds for delivering talks or leading groups is important. The backdrop helps to frame remarks.

Barack Obama has shown considerable skill in using props and staging to reinforce his messages. When he first announced his bid for the White House on February 10, 2007, for instance, he delivered his remarks in Springfield, Illinois, which naturally evoked memories of the lauded U.S. president Abraham Lincoln. Obama fixed attention on the significance of the setting, stating:

It was here, in Springfield, where north, south, east, and west come together that I was reminded of the essential decency of the American people—where I came to believe that through this decency, we can build a more hopeful America.

And that is why, in the shadow of the Old State Capitol, where Lincoln once called on a divided house to stand together, where common hopes and common dreams still live, I stand before you today to announce my candidacy for president of the United States.

I recognize there is a certain presumptuousness—a certain audacity—to this announcement. I know I haven't spent a lot of time learning the ways of Washington. But I've been there long enough to know that the ways of Washington must change.

The genius of our founders is that they designed a system of government that can be changed. And we should take heart, because we've changed this country before. In the face of tyranny, a band of patriots brought an empire to its knees. In the face of secession, we unified a nation and set the captives free. In the face of Depression, we put people back to work and lifted millions out of poverty. We welcomed immigrants to our shores, we opened railroads to the west, we landed a man on the moon, and we heard a King's call to let justice roll down like water, and righteousness like a mighty stream.

Each and every time, a new generation has risen up and done what's needed to be done. Today we are called once more—and it is time for our generation to answer that call.

For that is our unyielding faith—that in the face of impossible odds, people who love their country can change it.

That's what Abraham Lincoln understood. He had his doubts. He had his defeats. He had his setbacks. But through his will and his words, he moved a nation and helped free a people. It is because of the millions who rallied to his cause that we are no longer divided, North and South, slave and free. It is because men and women of every race, from every walk of life, continued to march for freedom long after Lincoln was laid to rest, that today we have the chance to face the challenges of this millennium together, as one people—as Americans.[1]

Similarly, when addressing the Reverend Jeremiah Wright controversy, Obama carefully considered the nonverbal messages he would be sending. Given his association with the controversial minister, Obama needed to address the incendiary words of Reverend Wright, which were perceived by many Americans to be racist and contrary to the values Obama espouses. Obama's association with Wright threatened the very foundation of his candidacy. Obama delivered his remarks from a lectern flanked by large American flags. While denouncing the divisive words of Reverend Wright, the large flags in back of Obama reinforced the notion that he is a loyal, patriotic American. The backdrop helped frame his remarks and sent a positive message.

⇥ BEGINNING STRONG ⇤

Another communication practice that helps Barack Obama earn trust and confidence is his ability to start "strong." By this, I mean he begins his talks in ways that tap into the prevailing mood, lighten any tensions, and focus attention. There are many ways to start strong—a moving quotation, a vivid anecdote, a light-hearted joke, a direct statement about the topic of the discussion, to name a few.

Given his consistency with strong starts, Obama seems keenly aware that if leaders begin their remarks in a weak manner, they will need to spend too much time recovering, trying to persuade people to give them another look. In practice, his motto could be characterized as, "Get off on the right foot the first time." Obama's achievements testify to the positive impact of catching attention early and steering audience focus to the most important themes. Consider, for example, Obama's win of the North Carolina primary. He used his beginning remarks to draw attention to the momentum of his campaign. He stated:

> You know, some were saying that North Carolina would be a game-changer in this election. But today, what North Carolina decided is that the only game that needs changing is the one in Washington, DC.
>
> I want to start by congratulating Senator Clinton on her victory in the state of Indiana. And I want to thank the people of North Carolina for giving us a victory in a big state, a swing state, and a state where we will compete to win if I am the Democratic nominee for president of the United States.

When this campaign began, Washington didn't give us much of a chance. But because you came out in the bitter cold, and knocked on doors, and enlisted your friends and neighbors in this cause; because you stood up to the cynics and the doubters and the naysayers when we were up and when we were down; because you still believe that this is our moment, and our time, for change—tonight we stand less than two hundred delegates away from securing the Democratic nomination for president of the United States.[2]

Even in the light of defeat, Obama skillfully chooses opening words. Consider, for instance, his remarks following his loss of the Pennsylvania primary. He projected that loss as a "win-because-we-narrowed-the-margin" situation:

I want to start by congratulating Senator Clinton on her victory tonight, and I want to thank the hundreds of thousands of Pennsylvanians who stood with our campaign today.

There were a lot of folks who didn't think we could make this a close race when it started. But we worked hard, and we traveled across the state to big cities and small towns, to factory floors, and VFW halls. And now, six weeks later, we closed the gap. We rallied people of every age and race and background to our cause. And whether they were inspired for the first time or for the first time in a long time, we registered a record number of voters who will lead our party to victory in November.[3]

Obama is so aware of the importance of beginning strong that when put in awkward positions unexpectedly, he makes sure to reset the tone of the conversation before proceeding with his remarks. A notable example of this occurred in December 2006 when Barack Obama appeared before a group of 2,000 Christians at a conference on HIV/AIDS at Saddleback Church in southern California. Another politician speaking at the same event, Senator Sam Brownback, spoke minutes before Obama. Standing on the church podium, Senator Brownback began his remarks to the primarily Caucasian audience by mentioning that he and Senator Obama had both recently addressed the National Association for the Advancement of Colored People (NAACP) and that, "They were very polite to me, but I think they kind of wondered 'Who's this guy from Kansas?'" Brownback complained that, by contrast, the NAACP and its audience had treated Obama like a rock star and Brownback seemed to imply that the difference was racial. He turned to Obama, seated behind him on the podium, and joked that he believed the tables were now turned, saying, "Welcome to *my* house."

Sitting in the room, I recall the shock that registered with many people in the audience. Barack Obama is a Christian, and we were sitting in a church! Brownback's comment seemed, rightly or wrongly, racially charged; it suggested that even though Obama was Christian, the church was not his house because the majority of people in the audience were white. It is very possible to argue that Brownback did not, in fact, intend this meaning and only referred to the audience's conservative bent, or that he misspoke, but the words were highly insulting and placed Senator Obama in a very awkward position.

When Brownback finished his speech minutes later and Obama moved to the lectern, many audience members seemed to hold their breaths, wondering if Obama would address the insult. It was no secret that some isolated evangelicals had been upset to learn that Obama would be appearing at the event and had sought to have him uninvited. Obama began by offering greetings from his church, underscoring quite intentionally that he was Christian. He then proceeded to offer Brownback compliments and more compliments. To my recollection, Obama spoke about how it was an honor to work with Senator Brownback on so many important issues and he praised Brownback's leadership. He went on at some length—a truly gracious beginning in light of the insult he had just received.

Then Obama did something quite brilliant. Before he proceeded to start his speech, he took the opportunity—having placed himself on the moral high ground by refusing to come out swinging—to turn to Senator Brownback who was seated at the back of the church podium. Obama smiled and said, "There is one thing I've got to say, Sam. This is my house, too! This is *God's* house."

The crowd erupted in applause. "I just wanted to be clear!" Obama said, riding the wave of support. Obama had set the record straight. Had he not, he would have started "weak" and proceeded forward in a highly compromised position, which could have undercut his speech. Instead, he successfully recast the dialogue and proceeded with a well-received talk.

CONVEYING ADMIRABLE ETHICS— DEVELOPING TEFLON

Finally, making certain to convey admirable ethics is an important way to earn trust and confidence. When a leader succeeds in conveying strong ethics and substantiates those ethics consistently through subsequent deeds, people begin to have great faith in their character and choices. Conveying strong ethics also has the added benefit of helping to "develop Teflon"—that is, a leader can build such an excellent ethical reputation that accusations and controversy "bounce off" of them rather than stick. When controversy arises, there is a greater likelihood that people will respond by thinking, "No, that is not who I have seen all this time." They are more likely to await an explanation and give a leader a chance.

In his public pronouncements, Barack Obama takes opportunities to convey his high ethical standards and commitment to principled values. Consider his remarks during his 2007 announcement for president in Springfield, Illinois:

[L]et me tell you how I came to be here. As most of you know, I am not a native of this great state. I moved to Illinois over two decades ago. I was a young man then, just a year out of college; I knew no one in Chicago, was without money or family connections. But a group of churches had offered me a job as a community organizer for $13,000 a year. And I accepted the job, sight unseen, motivated then by a single, simple, powerful idea—that I might play a small part in building a better America.

My work took me to some of Chicago's poorest neighborhoods. I joined with pastors and laypeople to deal with communities that had been ravaged by plant closings. I saw that the problems people faced weren't simply local in nature—that the decision to close a steel mill was made by distant executives; that the lack of textbooks and computers in schools could be traced to the skewed priorities of politicians a thousand miles away; and that when a child turns to violence, there's a hole in his heart no government alone can fill.

It was in these neighborhoods that I received the best education I ever had and where I learned the true meaning of my Christian faith.

After three years of this work, I went to law school because I wanted to understand how the law should work for those in need. I became a civil rights lawyer and taught constitutional law, and after a time, I came to understand that our cherished rights of liberty and equality depend on the active participation of an awakened electorate. It was with these ideas in mind that I arrived in this capital city as a state senator.

It was here, in Springfield, where I saw all that is America converge—farmers and teachers, businessmen and laborers, all of them with a story to tell, all of them seeking a seat at the table, all of them clamoring to be heard. I made lasting friendships here—friends that I see in the audience today.

It was here we learned to disagree without being disagreeable—that it's possible to compromise so long as you know those principles that can never be compromised; and that so long as we're willing to listen to each other, we can assume the best in people instead of the worst.[4]

In offering this short summary of his life choices, Obama underscored his principled values, morality, and commitment to community.

Similarly, Obama conveys admirable ethics by taking care in how he criticizes his opponents. When criticizing presidential candidate John McCain, for instance, he usually took care to first affirm McCain's service to the country. This helped him avoid an image of mudslinging. For instance, Obama said:

> In just a few short months, the Republican party will arrive in St. Paul with a very different agenda. They will come here to nominate John McCain, a man who has served this country heroically. I honor that service, and I respect his many accomplishments, even if he chooses to deny mine. My differences with him are not personal; they are with the policies he has proposed in this campaign.[5]

Obama's care in conveying strong ethics helped him to weather storms and to build his historic campaign around themes such as "leadership you can trust," and "change you can believe in."

⇥ WHAT WE'VE LEARNED—PRACTICES FOR ⇤ EARNING TRUST AND CONFIDENCE

Given Obama's tremendous success, leaders have much to learn from the way he uses excellent communication practices to earn the trust and confidence of others. We have seen that charisma plays a role in earning trust and confidence. People know charisma when they see it—that certain fire in the eye, passion and command. Charisma helps leaders energize and motivate others. Image and body language are also important for forming strong first impressions. Adept leaders capitalize on that first defining moment. Through skillful use of body movement and image, they start a two-way dialogue of sorts, making excellent impressions that last. This helps establish a firm foundation for commanding authority and wielding leadership.

Notable second impressions can reinforce strong first impressions. Through voice, intonation and skillful use of gestures, effective communicators underscore their confidence, self-assuredness, and worthiness as a leader. Effective communicators also bear in mind that how they say their words can give great potency to their remarks. They leverage excellent use of voice and intonation. Similarly, gestures serve as their tools, becoming fluid extensions of their spoken words, animating their dialogue and bringing greater impact to their pronouncements.

Strong communicators remember the importance of props and staging in sending sub-messages that reinforce key themes. They make efforts to "start strong" with their remarks, tapping into the prevailing mood and ensuring they begin their dialogues on favorable footing. Additionally, exceptional communicators take opportunities to convey their strong ethics, deepening a basis for trust and confidence that can bring benefits well into the future.

CHAPTER 3

BREAKING DOWN BARRIERS

Back in 2004, the notion of a 2008 Obama quest for the U.S. presidency would have been termed "improbable" at best. Many Americans would have scoffed, "He'll never get past his name!" The last name that sounds like "Osama;" that middle name, Hussein. Not to mention his race. Yet by 2008, Barack Obama was widely hailed as "a world-transforming, redemptive figure"[1] with a strong bid for the White House, whose victory might help heal a world long divided between white-black, North-South, rich-poor. How did Barack Obama manage to break down barriers that could have served as insurmountable obstacles to many other aspiring leaders?

One of the answers lies in Obama's distinguished ability to use communication to bring people together despite their differences and to establish common ground. The ability to unite people, build camaraderie, and promote a sense of shared goals is vital for every highly successful leader. Obama's skill in this area is particularly deep, as manifested by the magnitude of his political achievements. His success in claiming the 2008 Democratic nomination for president ranks as exceptional by way of world history. In the U.S. context alone, it remains remarkable how Obama managed to unite such a highly diverse coalition, which includes white-collar workers, blue-collar workers, students, soccer moms, and entrepreneurs of all races and ages. Obama put forth the message many times that, "this election is not between regions or religions or genders. It's not about rich versus poor; young versus old; and it is not about black versus white. It is about the past versus the future."[2] But how was he been able to cast aside the old divisions? This chapter explores the specific communication practices that enabled Barack Obama to successfully tear down barriers and forge ties to many disparate groups.

ACHIEVING TRANSCENDENCE

Barack Obama's highly effective communication practices have allowed him to achieve a high level of "transcendence." Obama has alluded to this himself, as he has insisted on many occasions that once people get to know him, they usually "come around." And how do people "get to know him"? Oration. Speeches. Public remarks. Because Obama's communication is so highly effective, his support has grown exponentially.

Several specific communication practices help account for Obama's success in inspiring a diverse set of people to band together, focusing not on their differences but on their commonalities. There are valuable lessons to be learned as we examine how Obama acknowledges differences but focuses on shared values, dreams, histories, and experiences; and the way he peppers his remarks with words that resonate, pulling from a powerful lexicon of political rhetoric, shared principles, biblical truths, and words of celebrated American icons. Below, we explore Obama's effective communication techniques.

⇉ ACKNOWLEDGING THE ELEPHANT IN THE ROOM ⇇

Barack Obama has achieved tremendous success in shattering conventional wisdom and breaking historic barriers. In 2004, Obama pointed to several sources of his success, explaining why many people considered him an attractive candidate and convention speaker. He noted the way he had won the Illinois U.S. senate primary election months earlier. "We defied conventional wisdom about where votes come from because the assumption is, whites won't vote for blacks, or suburban folks won't vote for city people, or downstate won't vote for upstate. . . . We were able to put together a coalition that said, you know, people are willing to give anybody a shot if they're speaking to them in a way that makes sense."[3] Obama also reiterated subsequently that people "are more interested in the message than the color of the messenger."[4]

But many leaders have failed in efforts to build such broad coalitions in the past. Obama's success involved more than good luck. He employs specific communication practices that have helped him to tear down obstacles and forge ties. One such practice: Obama openly acknowledges sources of potential discomfort early on. When he begins his public remarks, he often seems to act according to the principle, "If there's an elephant in the room, acknowledge it."

For Obama, the elephants in the room often include his race, his "funny name," and the fact that his father comes from a developing part of the world and once lived in a hut. Given the history of race in the United States, this background might have presented an insurmountable obstacle for leaders less skilled than Obama.

Rather than ignoring these issues of potential discomfort, Obama is adept at acknowledging them head-on, often with touches of humor. He once joked, for instance, that all too often people found his name confusing and accidentally called him by other, more familiar names like "Alabama" or "Yo mama."[5] Obama also referred to himself as "a skinny kid with a funny name." As he acknowledged at the 2004 convention, "Let's face it, my presence on this stage is pretty unlikely." Obama's comfort in acknowledging the elephants in a room eases the comfort of those to whom he speaks. This, in turn, sets him free to redirect attention skillfully to areas of common ground.

Obama shows that as a public speaker, it is useful to try to acknowledge sources of potential discomfort early on and in a forthright manner. Doing so can aid a quest to move beyond issues that divide in order to focus on efforts to build ties and strengthen common ground.

STRESSING COMMON DREAMS AND VALUES

As Obama adeptly recasts the dialogue to stress commonalities rather than differences, he focuses on key aspects such as shared dreams and values. Consider this example:

[I] finally took my first trip to his tiny village in Kenya and asked my grandmother if there was anything left from [*my father*]. She opened a trunk and took out a stack of letters, which she handed to me.

There were more than thirty of them, all handwritten by my father, all addressed to colleges and universities across America, all filled with *the hope of a young man who dreamed of more for his life.* And his *prayer was answered* when he was brought over to study in this country.[6] [*Emphases provided*]

In these remarks, Obama focuses our attention on the hope of a young man and the prayers that were answered—things to which average Americans can relate. The aspects of his father's experience that would serve to separate Obama from most Americans—the hut and Kenya—fade in our mind as Obama steers our attention to the areas of commonality. Aspiring leaders can learn much from this. When preparing remarks, consider this: What common ground elements can you bring to the fore to establish strong ties to your audience? How can you skillfully direct attention to areas of common ground rather than keep the audience focused on elements that divide?

We can also learn much from Obama's skill in establishing common ground among diverse sets of people as we observe how he focuses away from traditional societal divisions—class, race, ethnicity, region, and religion—and focuses toward shared values and dreams. On March 18, 2004, the *New York Times* quoted Obama as saying, "I have an unusual name and an exotic background, but my values are essentially American values."[7] Obama promotes this theme vigorously and uses shared values—such as strong work ethic, belief in the American dream, and desire for education—as the basis for relating to a broad array of the American public. Consider his remarks at the Associated Press annual luncheon in Washington, DC, in April 2008:

It doesn't matter if they're Democrats or Republicans; whether they're from the smallest towns or the biggest cities; whether they hunt or they don't; whether they go to church, or temple, or mosque, or not. We may come from different places and have different stories, but we share common hopes and one very American dream.

That is the dream I am running to help restore in this election. If I get the chance, that is what I'll be talking about from now until November. That is the choice that I'll offer the American people—four more years of what we had for the last eight, or fundamental change in Washington.

People may be bitter about their leaders and the state of our politics, but beneath that they are hopeful about what's possible in America. That's why they leave their homes on their day off, or their jobs after a long day of work, and travel—sometimes for miles, sometimes in the bitter cold—to attend a rally or a town hall meeting held by Senator Clinton, or Senator McCain, or myself. Because they believe that we can change things. Because they believe in that dream.

I know something about that dream. I wasn't born into a lot of money. I was raised by a single mother with the help of my grandparents, who grew up in small-town Kansas, went to school on the GI Bill, and bought their home through an FHA loan. My mother had to use food stamps at one point, but she still made sure that, through scholarships, I got a chance to go to some of the best schools around, which helped me get into some of the best colleges around, which gave me loans that Michelle and I just finished paying not all that many years ago.

In other words, my story is a quintessentially American story. It's the same story that has made this country a beacon for the world—a story of struggle and sacrifice on the part of my forebearers and a story of overcoming great odds. I carry that story with me each and every day. It's why I wake up every day and do this, and it's why I continue to hold such hope for the future of a country where the dreams of its people have always been possible.[8]

In his remarks above, Obama again joins himself firmly to the diverse audience he is addressing as he draws attention to their shared American dream. Similarly, in the example below, Obama solidifies his ties to a diverse set of Americans as he describes his family's pursuit of the American dream and their commitment to commendable values—hard work and dedication:

This is the country that gave my grandfather a chance to go to college on the GI Bill when he came home from World War II; a country that gave him and my grandmother the chance to buy their first home with a loan from the government.

This is the country that made it possible for my mother—a single parent who had to go on food stamps at one point—to send my sister and me to the best schools in the country on scholarships.

This is the country that allowed my father-in-law—a city worker at a South Side water filtration plant—to provide for his wife and two children on a single salary. This is a man who was diagnosed at age thirty with multiple sclerosis—who relied on a walker to get himself to work. And yet, every day he went, and he labored, and he sent my wife and her brother to one of the best colleges in the nation. It was a job that didn't just give him a paycheck, but a sense of dignity and self-worth. It was an America that didn't just reward wealth, but the work and the workers who created it.[9]

As political commentator Jamal Simmons noted on June 3, 2008, Obama has succeeded in presenting his life story as a "uniquely American story. . . . Like Bill Clinton's story, Ronald Reagan's story, Harry Truman's story. . . ."[10] The *New York Times* concurred on July 28, 2004, indicating that Obama tells "a classic American story of immigration, hope, striving and opportunity." Given his excellent communication practices, Obama has portrayed his life's tale as that of an American with humble beginnings making his way to extraordinary success. This has helped him connect with audiences; his life story is viewed as a classic story and it has endeared Obama to millions of Americans.

⇥ DRAWING ATTENTION TO SHARED HISTORY ⇤

Obama's emphasis on common dreams—particularly the American dream—and shared values has endeared him to millions of Americans. When possible, Obama also stresses shared history as a way of relating to audiences. Think about this example:

I am the son of a black man from Kenya and a white woman from Kansas. I was raised with the help of a white grandfather who survived a *Depression* to serve in *Patton's army during World War II* and a white grandmother who worked on a *bomber assembly line at Fort Leavenworth* while he was overseas. I've gone to some of the best schools in America and lived in one of the world's poorest nations. I am married to a black American who carries within her the *blood of slaves* and *slaveowners*—an inheritance we pass on to our two precious daughters. I have brothers, sisters, nieces, nephews, uncles, and cousins of every race and every hue, scattered across three continents, and for as long as I live, I will never forget that in no other country on Earth is my story even possible.

It's a story that hasn't made me the most conventional candidate. But it is a story that has seared into my genetic makeup the idea that this nation is more than the sum of its parts—*that out of many, we are truly one.*[11] [*Emphases provided*]

While Obama acknowledges that his father was a Kenyan, he casts his father's story as a typical American immigrant story characterized by great hope for a better future, education, hard work, and the attainment of the American dream. Obama's references to shared history—the Depression, Patton's army and World War II, and the bomber assembly line at Fort Leavenworth—help him do this convincingly. These familiar historical references help Obama establish himself as being "just like any other American." He successfully directs the conversation away from his "funny" name and unorthodox upbringing to the many ties that bind. In doing so, Obama projects himself as firmly a part of the "we," part of the same team as most Americans, striving for the same goals.

Consider another example, in which the specific details Obama provides help form connections with a diverse audience:

> [W]hat I learned much later is that part of what made it possible for [my father to come to the United States] was an effort by the young senator from Massachusetts at the time, John F. Kennedy, and by a grant from the Kennedy Foundation to help Kenyan students pay for travel. So it is partly because of their generosity that my father came to this country, and because he did, I stand before you today—inspired by America's past, filled with hope for America's future, and determined to do my part in writing our next great chapter.[12]

In these comments, Obama uses an outstanding choice of detail to tie himself firmly to the American audience; he refers to one of the most famous American political families, taps into patriotic sentiments as he refers to the "generosity" of an American, and projects himself as "inspired by America's past" while also representing its future.

Similarly, Obama drew attention to shared history as a means of building links to an audience at the Kennedy endorsement event in Washington, DC, in January 2008. He commented:

> Today isn't just about politics for me. It's personal. I was too young to remember John Kennedy, and I was just a child when Robert Kennedy ran for president. But in the stories

I heard growing up, I saw how my grandparents and mother spoke about them and about that period in our nation's life—as a time of great hope and achievement. And I think my own sense of what's possible in this country comes in part from what they said America was like in the days of John and Robert Kennedy.

I believe that's true for millions of Americans. I've seen it in offices in this city where portraits of John and Robert hang on office walls or collections of their speeches sit on bookshelves. And I've seen it in my travels all across this country. Because no matter where I go or who I talk to, one thing I can say for certain is *that the dream has never died.*

The dream lives on in the older folks I meet who remember what America once was and know what America can be once again. It lives on in the young people who've only seen John or Robert Kennedy on TV, but are ready to answer their call.

It lives on in those Americans who refuse to be deterred by the scale of the challenges we face, who know, as President Kennedy said at this university, that "no problem of human destiny is beyond human beings."

And it lives on in those Americans—young and old, rich and poor, black and white, Latino and Asian—who are tired of a politics that divide us and want to recapture the sense of common purpose that we had when John Kennedy was president.

That is the dream *we hold in our hearts.* That is the kind of leadership we need in this country. And that is the kind of leadership I intend to offer as president.[13] [*Emphases provided*]

These familiar themes have enabled Obama to break down barriers and build bridges. In garnering political support, he has cast aside traditional divisions and laid in their place other bases for uniting—shared values and shared history—that have enabled him to motivate unprecedented numbers of people.

⇥ ILLUMINATING SHARED EXPERIENCES ⇤

Another important lesson of Obama's outstanding communication style is how he leverages shared experiences to build rapport and a strong sense of camaraderie. As we have seen, when addressing an audience, Obama searches out the common ground and deliberately draws attention to it. At times, this common ground may be limited to tangential experiences. But Obama manages to leverage even tangential experiences, using them to forge a foundation upon which to relate to an audience. Consider the example below, when Obama spoke before a group of working women. Clearly, Obama is not a working woman! But he took time to consider how he could relate to the group. The relevant questions he seemed to consider beforehand included: What is the basis of our common experiences? How can I elaborate on those common experiences—even if they are only tangential—in establishing a firm connection to the audience? Obama creates a firm connection magnificently as he uses his experience as the son of a working woman and as the husband of a working woman to illuminate common ground:

> It's great to be back in New Mexico and to have this opportunity to discuss some of the challenges that working women are facing. Because I would not be standing before

you today as a candidate for president of the United States if it weren't for working women.

I am here because of my mother, a single mom who put herself through school, followed her passion for helping others, and raised my sister and me to believe that in America there are no barriers to success if you're willing to work for it.

I am here because of my grandmother, who helped raised me. She worked during World War II on a bomber assembly line—she was Rosie the Riveter. Then, even though she never got more than a high school diploma, she worked her way up from her start as a secretary at a bank and ended up being the financial rock for our entire family when I was growing up.

And I am here because of my wife, Michelle, the rock of the Obama family, who worked her way up from modest roots on the South Side of Chicago, and who has juggled jobs and parenting with more skill and grace than anyone I know. Now Michelle and I want our two daughters to grow up in an America where they have the freedom and opportunity to live their dreams and raise their own families.[14]

In another example, Obama gives a speech before a metropolitan group in Florida. Obama calculated again how he could relate to the audience. What sorts of experiences or histories did they share? How could he elaborate in a way that would create a lucid picture of himself as a candidate who understands their situation, their challenges, their needs? Although the group is based in Miami, Florida, Obama pulls effectively from his experience as an organizer in Chicago, Illinois, establishing common ground.

This is something of a homecoming for me. Because while I stand here today as a candidate for president of the United States, I will never forget that the most important experience in my life came when I was doing what you do each day—working at the local level to bring about change in our communities.

As some of you may know, after college I went to work with a group of churches as a community organizer in Chicago so I could help lift up neighborhoods that were struggling after the local steel plants closed. And it taught me a fundamental truth that I carry with me to this day— that in this country, change comes not from the top down, but from the bottom up.[15]

For leaders aspiring to diminish perceived areas of division and to expand common ground, Obama's successes demonstrate the value of taking time to identify the many bases that might serve as common ground areas. Do your listeners share common histories? Common values? Common experiences? Common goals? Shine a light on the areas of commonalities in order to build bridges and unite disparate groups of people.

EMPLOYING WORDS THAT RESONATE: THE HISTORICAL AND POLITICAL LEXICON

We have seen above how Obama skillfully creates a sense of "we-ness," making himself and the audience a part of the "we" as he elaborates on their common values, dreams, histories, and experiences. Buttressing this, Obama peppers his remarks with words that resonate with his audiences. At times, he pulls those appropriate words from the American political lexicon, drawing on our shared, cherished sociopolitical values. At times, he draws on valued principles and biblical truths. At other times, he refers to the words of American iconic figures in order to underscore his message.

Consider this example, when Obama responds to the fiery and divisive comments of Reverend Jeremiah Wright, which threatened to undercut Obama's assertions that he stood for a united America. Obama chose to draw on America's rich history of political rhetoric, using words from the Declaration of Independence that resonated with the audience. Referring to the Declaration of Independence was akin to pouring buckets full of water on a fire, quenching its flames. In the single opening sentence below, Obama affirmed his patriotism and communicated his unwavering support of the ideals of unity:

"*We the people, in order to form a more perfect union.*"
      Two hundred and twenty-one years ago, in a hall that still stands across the street, a group of men gathered and, with these simple words, launched America's improbable experiment in democracy. Farmers and scholars; statesmen and patriots who had traveled across an ocean to escape tyranny and persecution finally made real their declaration of independence at a Philadelphia convention that lasted through the spring of 1787.
      The document they produced was eventually signed but ultimately unfinished. It was stained by this nation's original sin of slavery, a question that divided the colonies and brought the convention to a stalemate until the founders chose to allow the slave trade to continue for at least twenty

more years and to leave any final resolution to future generations.

Of course, the answer to the slavery question was already embedded within our Constitution—a constitution that had at is very core the ideal of equal citizenship under the law; a constitution that promised its people liberty, and justice, and a union that could be and should be perfected over time.

And yet words on a parchment would not be enough to deliver slaves from bondage or provide men and women of every color and creed their full rights and obligations as citizens of the United States. What would be needed were Americans in successive generations who were willing to do their part—through protests and struggle, on the streets and in the courts, through a civil war and civil disobedience and always at great risk—to narrow that gap between the promise of our ideals and the reality of their time.

This was one of the tasks we set forth at the beginning of this campaign—to continue the long march of those who came before us, a march for a more just, more equal, more free, more caring, and more prosperous America. I chose to run for the presidency at this moment in history because I believe deeply that we cannot solve the challenges of our time unless we solve them together—unless we perfect our union by understanding that we may have different stories, but we hold common hopes; that we may not look the same and we may not have come from the same place, but we all want to move in the same direction—towards a better future for our children and our grandchildren.

This belief comes from my unyielding faith in the decency and generosity of the American people. [*Emphases added*]

In this speech, Obama roots himself firmly as a part of the "we" and conveys that the treasured historic principles that guided the United States continue forward and will lead us into a secure future.

⇥ USING WORDS THAT RESONATE— ⇤ BIBLICAL TRUTHS

Another practice that allows Obama to shatter barriers and construct ties effectively is his tendency to reference biblical words. Obama, a Christian whose faith is dear to him, often sprinkles his public remarks with words that evoke faith among other Christians: *faith in things not seen; I am my brother's keeper.* Many people cherish these biblical truths and principles. For broad segments of the American population, Obama's use of such language establishes a high level of connectedness. The verses are familiar to many ears and resonate in many hearts. Referring to them helps to build bridges. Just consider this excerpt from Obama's 2004 Democratic Convention keynote address:

For alongside our famous individualism, there's another ingredient in the American saga.

A belief that we are connected as one people. If there's a child on the South Side of Chicago who can't read, that matters to me, even if it's not my child. If there's a senior citizen somewhere who can't pay for her prescription and has to choose between medicine and the rent, that makes my life poorer, even if it's not my grandmother. If there's an Arab American family being rounded up without benefit of an attorney or due process, that threatens my civil liberties. It's that fundamental belief—*I am my brother's keeper, I am my sister's keeper*—that makes this country work. It's what allows us to pursue our individual dreams, yet still come together as a single American family. "E pluribus unum." Out of many, one.[16] [*Emphases provided*]

Similarly, in his seminal "A More Perfect Union" speech in Philadelphia in March 2008, Obama's biblical references served him well:

In the end, then, what is called for is nothing more and nothing less than what all the world's great religions demand—*that we do unto others as we would have them do unto us*. Let us be *our brother's keeper*, *Scripture tells us. Let us be our sister's keeper*. Let us find that common stake we all have in one another, and let our politics reflect that spirit as well."[17] [*Emphases provided*]

⇥ LEVERAGING OTHER PEOPLE'S WORDS ⇤

Drawing on the words of lauded American icons has also helped Barack Obama establish linkages to audiences. The icons he chooses are often well known to audiences, and their words are sometimes familiar. Referring to the words of carefully chosen icons or leaders helps establish an emotional connection to the audience. Consider this excerpt from Obama's January 2008 speech:

[O]n the eve of the bus boycotts in Montgomery, at a time when many were still doubtful about the possibilities of change, a time when those in the black community mistrusted themselves, and at times mistrusted each other, King inspired with words not of anger, but of an urgency that still speaks to us today:

"Unity is the great need of the hour" is what King said. Unity is how we shall overcome.

What Dr. King understood is that if just one person chose to walk instead of ride the bus, those walls of oppression would not be moved. But maybe if a few more walked, the foundation might start to shake. If a few more women were willing to do what Rosa Parks had done, maybe the cracks would start to show. If teenagers took freedom rides from North to South, maybe a few bricks would come loose. Maybe if white folks marched because they had come to understand that their freedom too was at stake in the impending battle, the wall would begin to sway. And if enough Americans were awakened to the injustice; if they joined together, North and South, rich and poor, Christian and Jew, then perhaps that wall would come tumbling down, and justice would flow like water, and righteousness like a mighty stream.

Unity is the great need of the hour—the great need of this hour.[18]

The poetry of King's words, along with his iconic stature, helps to yield an emotional impact for many listeners. By drawing on such words, Obama has on many occasions related to audiences with greater effectiveness. In another example, Obama references, with great effect, Martin Luther King Jr.'s eloquent words, "the arc of the moral universe is long but it bends toward justice":

> Through his faith, courage, and wisdom, Dr. Martin Luther King Jr. moved an entire nation. He preached the gospel of brotherhood; of equality and justice. That's the cause for which he lived—and for which he died forty years ago today . . .
>
> [I] think it's worth reflecting on what Dr. King was doing in Memphis, when he stepped onto that motel balcony on his way out for dinner. . . .
>
> And what he was doing was standing up for struggling sanitation workers. For years, these workers had served their city without complaint, picking up other people's trash for little pay and even less respect. Passersby would call them "walking buzzards," and, in the segregated South, most were forced to use separate drinking fountains and bathrooms.
>
> . . . [O]n the eve of his death, Dr. King gave a sermon in Memphis about what the movement there meant to him and to America. And in tones that would prove eerily prophetic, Dr. King said that despite the threats he'd received, he didn't fear any man, because he had been there when Birmingham aroused the conscience of this nation. And he'd been there to see the students stand up for freedom by sitting in at lunch counters. And he'd been there in Memphis when it was dark enough to see the stars, to see the community coming together around a common pur-

pose. So Dr. King had been to the mountaintop. He had seen the Promised Land. And while he knew somewhere deep in his bones that he would not get there with us, he knew that we would get there.

He knew it because he had seen that Americans have "the capacity," as he said that night, "to project the 'I' into the 'thou.'" To recognize that no matter what the color of our skin, no matter what faith we practice, no matter how much money we have, no matter whether we are sanitation workers or United States senators, we all have a stake in one another, we are our brother's keeper, we are our sister's keeper, and "either we go up together, or we go down together."

And when he was killed the following day, it left a wound on the soul of our nation that has yet to fully heal. . . . That is why the great need of this hour is much the same as it was when Dr. King delivered his sermon in Memphis. We have to recognize that while we each have a different past, we all share the same hopes for the future—that we'll be able to find a job that pays a decent wage, that there will be affordable health care when we get sick, that we'll be able to send our kids to college, and that after a lifetime of hard work we'll be able to retire with security. They're common hopes, modest dreams. And they're at the heart of the struggle for freedom, dignity, and humanity that Dr. King began, and that it is our task to complete.

You know, Dr. King once said that the arc of the moral universe is long, but that it bends toward justice. But what he also knew was that it doesn't bend on its own. It bends because each of us puts our hands on that arc and bends it in the direction of justice.

So on this day of all days *let's each do our part to bend that arc.*

Let's bend that arc toward justice.

Let's bend that arc toward opportunity.

Let's bend that arc toward prosperity for all.

And if we can do that and march together—as one nation and one people—then we won't just be keeping faith with what Dr. King lived and died for. We'll be making real the words of Amos that he invoked so often, and "let justice roll down like water and righteousness like a mighty stream."[19] [*Emphases provided*]

Obama's highly effective communication practices enable him to unite a broad range of disparate groups within American society, resulting in one of the largest and most significant grassroots political movements in recent years. For leaders aspiring to steer attention away from factors that divide listeners toward factors that unite them, Obama demonstrates that words that resonate—reflecting common values, principles, beliefs, tradition and history—can be used to build a greater sense of unity.

⇥ WHAT WE'VE LEARNED—PRACTICES FOR ⇤ BREAKING DOWN BARRIERS

Leaders have much to learn from the way Barack Obama breaks down barriers and establishes common ground among diverse sets of people. Obama has shown he can transcend traditional divisions of race, ethnicity, age, gender, religion, and region. He is adept at uniting disparate people, building camaraderie, and establishing a sense of shared goals. To do this, we have seen the importance of acknowledging "elephants in the room." Acknowledging potential issues of discomfort helps to ease tensions and enables leaders to re-focus attention on areas of common ground. Leaders should seek to be forthright in acknowledging areas of potential discomfort early on and with forthrightness, and should proceed to focus away from sources of division and toward sources of commonalities. The aim is to recast the dialogue, steering attention in ways that promote a sense that listeners are on the same team, striving for the same aims.

When illuminating common ground, it is helpful to reference common history, common values, and common experiences. It is also a best practice to employ words that resonate—well-chosen words reflecting time-tested principles, socio-political values, biblical truth, or a cherished lexicon of political rhetoric. Effective use of "other people's words" can also play a role. Leaders can focus when needed on iconic figures, those we all admire, incorporating references to their words wisely and using those references to create a connection, a sense of "we"-ness. When establishing common ground, referring to details about shared experiences, even tangential experiences, can also prove useful. When constructing public pronouncements, therefore, effective leaders assess the basis of their shared experiences with their audiences, identifying ways to highlight those commonalities to deepen a sense of connection, enhancing the power of their words.

CHAPTER 4

WINNING HEARTS AND MINDS

When fully harnessing the power of speaking with purpose and vision, outstanding orators can win hearts and minds, eliciting responses such as, "That was a powerful speech." "He understands." "She addressed all of my concerns."

Barack Obama has shown a notable ability to sway the hearts and minds of audiences. He knows how to wield communicative power in ways that move people and motivate them to follow his lead. He has inspired young generations of voters and reinvigorated older generations, spurring a historic grassroots campaign that trumped political wisdom about traditional divisions around racial, class, gender, and religious lines. His ability to sway a broad swath of the American public spurred new self-named cadres: Obama Mamas, Obamacans, adherents of Obama-nomics. What allows Barack Obama to connect so well with his audiences and makes oration one of his greatest strengths?

It is possible to glean important lessons from Obama's keen ability to adapt his remarks to the audience and topic at hand. He makes sure to know his audience, recognize their prevailing mood, and speak meaningfully to them about issues they most care about. Several other notable practices underlie Obama's skill in swaying hearts and minds. He acts according to the principle, "Keep things personal," employing details effectively and creating the feel of one-to-one conversation, making ample references to his personal experiences and leveraging the "I," "you," and "we" connection with skillful use of personal pronouns. The net effect: when Barack Obama speaks, the podium seems to disappear; Obama creates a two-way dialogue of sorts, as if he is standing near, speaking directly to listeners. Obama sways listeners as he speaks about issues of paramount importance to them and demonstrates understanding and empathy. He builds rapport. Given his communication style and substance, his audiences respond, feeling that they are a part of a "we," part of the same team, striving for the same goals.

⇥ KNOWING YOUR AUDIENCE ⇤

In order to win hearts and minds, it is necessary to know your audience and understand the circumstances its members face. Effective leaders not only know this information, but they also *convey* their understanding to the audience. They use language that captures the mood and addresses the audience's key concerns, grievances, and desires. Barack Obama has demonstrated an outstanding ability to connect with his audiences in this way. He acknowledges and addresses their prevailing moods and sentiments. The issues may vary—the economy, health care, education, the Iraq War. But in his comments, Obama shows skill in conveying to his audiences that he understands their perspectives and intends to address their concerns. Consider when Obama addressed the lack of optimism (some would say, outright cynicism) that some Americans have felt recently toward government and government officials:

I chose to run because I believed that the size of these challenges had outgrown the capacity of our broken and divided politics to solve them; because I believed that Americans of every political stripe were hungry for a new kind of politics, a politics that focused not just on how to win but why we should, a politics that focused on those values and ideals that we held in common as Americans; a politics that favored common sense over ideology, straight talk over spin.

Most of all, I believed in the power of the American people to be the real agents of change in this country because we are not as divided as our politics suggests; because we are a decent, generous people willing to work hard and sacrifice for future generations; and I was certain that if we could just mobilize our voices to challenge the special interests that dominate Washington and challenge ourselves to reach for something better, there was no problem we couldn't solve—no destiny we couldn't fulfill.

Ten months later, Iowa, you have vindicated that faith. You've come out in the blistering heat and the bitter cold not just to cheer, but to challenge—to ask the tough questions; to lift the hood and kick the tires; to serve as one place in America where someone who hasn't spent their life in the Washington spotlight can get a fair hearing.

You've earned the role you play in our democracy because no one takes it more seriously. And I believe that's true this year more than ever because, like me, you feel that same sense of urgency.[1]

In capturing the prevailing mood, Obama succeeded in connecting with his audience and advanced his goal of swaying hearts and minds. His remarks "hit home." For leaders seeking to use excellent communication to win hearts and minds, take time to know your audiences and to come to understand what they most want to hear about. Find ways to tap into the prevailing mood and speak meaningfully to them about the things they most care about.

⇥ KNOWING WHEN NOT TO ENUMERATE ⇤

When seeking to win hearts and minds—pursuing the aims of inspiring and motivating people—it is important to know when not to enumerate remarks. Strikingly, orators seeking to establish a strong emotional connection to listeners rarely enumerate their points. Numbering points, ideas, or themes is perceived as an emotion-dampener. Imagine the impression a speaker makes when beginning a discussion by saying, "Let me elaborate on four key components of my vision. First . . ." The talk will be perceived as formal, businesslike, distant, void of deep emotion, and less extemporaneous.

Certainly, enumeration has its place. It can be highly effective in business settings or in relatively formal settings such as church services. Many a professor, also, has been heard saying, "Let me elaborate on the three things that. . . ." But for the broader aim of capturing hearts and minds, enumeration represents a stifling format. If seeking to sway hearts and minds, it is often best to provide structure to remarks without the formality of enumeration.

Barack Obama adheres to this strain of thought. Rarely in recent years has he delivered speeches to public audiences in which enumeration found a notable place in the way he conveyed his comments. This is not to say that Obama offers speeches or remarks that are void of effective structure. Quite the opposite. Obama has adopted multiple techniques for providing great structure to his remarks without enumeration, preserving his ability to make a strong visceral connection to his audiences. Consider this example:

So this will not be easy. Make no mistake about what we're up against.

We are up against the belief that it's ok for lobbyists to dominate our government—that they are just part of the system in Washington. But we know that the undue influence of lobbyists is part of the problem, and this election is our chance to say that we're not going to let them stand in our way anymore.

We are up against the conventional thinking that says your ability to lead as president comes from longevity in Washington or proximity to the White House. But we know that real leadership is about candor, and judgment and the ability to rally Americans from all walks of life around a common purpose—a higher purpose.

We are up against decades of bitter partisanship that causes politicians to demonize their opponents instead of coming together to make college affordable or energy cleaner; it's the kind of partisanship where you're not even allowed to say that a Republican had an idea, even if it's one you never agreed with. That kind of politics is bad for our party, it's bad for our country, and this is our chance to end it once and for all.

We are up against the idea that it's acceptable to say anything and do anything to win an election. We know that this is exactly what's wrong with our politics; this is why people don't believe what their leaders say anymore; this is why they tune out. And this election is our chance to give the American people a reason to believe again.

And what we've seen in these last weeks is that we're also up against forces that are not the fault of any one campaign, but feed the habits that prevent us from being who we want to be as a nation. It's the politics that uses religion as a wedge and patriotism as a bludgeon. A politics that tells us that we have to think, act, and even vote within the confines of the categories that supposedly define us. The assumption that young people are apathetic. The assumption that Republicans won't cross over. The assumption that the wealthy care nothing for the poor and that the poor don't vote. The assumption that African Americans can't support the white candidate; whites can't support the African American candidate; blacks and Latinos can't come together.

But we are here tonight to say that this is not the America we believe in. I did not travel around this state over the last year and see a white South Carolina or a black South Carolina. I saw South Carolina. I saw crumbling schools that are stealing the future of black children and white children. I saw shuttered mills and homes for sale that once belonged to Americans from all walks of life, and men and women of every color and creed who serve together, and fight together, and bleed together under the same proud flag. I saw what America is, and I believe in what this country can be.

That is the country I see. That is the country you see. But now it is up to us to help the entire nation embrace this vision. Because in the end, we are not just up against the ingrained and destructive habits of Washington; we are also struggling against our own doubts, our own fears, and our own cynicism. The change we seek has always required great struggle and sacrifice. And so this is a battle in our own hearts and minds about what kind of country we want and how hard we're willing to work for it.[2]

In this example, Obama demonstrates that a message can be highly structured without sacrificing the personal touch. The way Obama frames his paragraphs—repeating, "We are up against"—serves as a source of structure, no enumeration needed.

For leaders aspiring to employ effective communication, think about whether enumeration will help you achieve your goal or hinder it. Consider the purpose of your talk and the venue, and choose to use or avoid enumeration accordingly.

⇥ EMPLOYING DETAILS EFFECTIVELY ⇤

Another way to capture hearts and minds is to speak meaningfully to the needs of listeners. Details matter. Important to listeners are the three Rs—recognizes, remembers, responsive. Listeners want assurance that the speaker *realizes* the circumstances they are facing, *remembers* the details of those circumstances enough to reference them, and will be *responsive* to those issues. In providing details, a speaker helps to answer questions that are often in the minds of audience members, such as "What do you *really* know about my life and my challenges? Do you care?" Details provide evidence of awareness and empathy.

Barack Obama is excellent at communicating to audiences that he is aware of their circumstances, understands those challenges, and is preparing to do something about them. In a practice he has improved over time, Obama often provides sufficient details to convey, "I offer this evidence that I understand and that I care." Consider this example:

> All across this state, you've shared with me your stories. And all too often they've been stories of struggle and hardship.
>
> I've heard from seniors who were betrayed by CEOs who dumped their pensions while pocketing bonuses and from those who still can't afford their prescriptions because Congress refused to negotiate with the drug companies for the cheapest available price.
>
> I've met Maytag workers who labored all their lives only to see their jobs shipped overseas; who now compete with their teenagers for $7-an-hour jobs at Wal-Mart.

I've spoken with teachers who are working at doughnut shops after school just to make ends meet; who are still digging into their own pockets to pay for school supplies.

Just two weeks ago, I heard a young woman in Cedar Rapids who told me she only gets three hours of sleep because she works the night shift after a full day of college and still can't afford health care for a sister with cerebral palsy. She spoke not with self-pity but with determination and wonders why the government isn't doing more to help her afford the education that will allow her to live out her dreams.

I've spoken to veterans who talk with pride about what they've accomplished in Afghanistan and Iraq, but who nevertheless think of those they've left behind and question the wisdom of our mission in Iraq; the mothers weeping in my arms over the memories of their sons; the disabled or homeless vets who wonder why their service has been forgotten.

And I've spoken to Americans in every corner of the state, patriots all, who wonder why we have allowed our standing in the world to decline so badly, so quickly. They know this has not made us safer. They know that we must never negotiate out of fear but that we must never fear to negotiate with our enemies as well as our friends. They are ashamed of Abu Ghraib and Guantanamo and warrantless wiretaps and ambiguity on torture. They love their country and want its cherished values and ideals restored.[3]

Imagine the difference, the flatness of the remarks, if Obama had simply stated, "I understand there are tough economic times right now. My new policy can help." There is more credibility and power to his words when he demonstrates a depth of knowledge through carefully chosen details. By adding more precise details—$7 an hour, a need to work after school—outstanding orators like Obama make greater strides toward winning hearts and minds.

For leaders aiming to strengthen their ability to use communication to win hearts and minds, take time to think about what detail can help you communicate to listeners that you recognize, remember, and will be responsive to the issues they most care about. Employing effective detail is a powerful tool in the communication process.

⇥ PERSONALIZING THE MESSAGE— ⇤ "I" AND EXPERIENCE

In using communication as a powerful tool, Barack Obama demonstrates that another important way to win hearts and minds is to personalize a message with skillful use of pronouns—the "I," "you," and "we" connection. Tapping into a prevailing mood is important, yes. Providing effective details is important, also. But sometimes it is easy to overlook what you, the speaker, believe specifically and the experiences that underpin those beliefs. Personalizing a message and referring to your own relevant experience help to personalize the message and to establish credibility. Your experiences help establish your authority. References to relevant experience, combined with skillful employment of "you," "I," and "we," help transmit the message that the speaker and the audience are part of the same team. It helps elicit the reaction, "He's been there; he knows." This, in turn, lays the foundation for swaying hearts and minds. Below, Obama demonstrates this practice:

> Finally, as *you and I* stand here today, know that there is a generation of children growing up on the mean streets and forgotten corners of this country who are slipping away from us as we speak. They walk down Corridors of Shame in rural South Carolina and sit in battered classrooms somewhere in East LA. They are overwhelmingly black and Latino and poor. And when they look around and see that no one has lifted a finger to fix their school since the nineteenth century; when they are pushed out the door at the sound of the last bell—some into a virtual war zone— is it any wonder they don't think their education is important? Is it any wonder that they are dropping out in rates we've never seen before?
>
> *I know* these children. *I know* their sense of hopelessness. *I began my career* over two decades ago as a community organizer on the streets of Chicago's South Side. And I worked with parents and teachers and local leaders to fight for their future. We set up after-school programs, and we even protested outside government offices so that we could get those who had dropped out into alternative schools. And in time, we changed futures.
>
> *And so while I know hopelessness, I also know* hope. *I know* that if we bring early education programs to these communities; if we stop waiting until high-school to address the dropout rate and start in earlier grades; if we bring in new,

qualified teachers; if we expand college outreach programs like GEAR UP and TRIO and fight to expand summer learning opportunities *like I've done* in the senate; if we do all this, we can make a difference in the lives of our children and the life of this country—not just in East LA or the South Side of Chicago, but here in Manchester, and suburban Boston, and rural Mississippi. *I know* we can. *I've seen* it happen. And *I will work* every day to do it again as your president.[4] [*Emphases provided*]

⇒ CONNECTING ONE TO ONE: "YOU" AND "I" ⇐

Combining references to "I" with references to "you" also personalizes a message, creating a greater sense of closeness. The distance between the podium and the audience seems to narrow. Whatever physical barriers are present (a lectern, for instance) become lesser obstacles. The speaker's words strike closer to the heart. Consider this:

> *My father* came from thousands of miles away, in Kenya, and went back there soon after I was born. *I spent* a childhood adrift. *I was raised* in Hawaii and Indonesia. *I lived* with my single mom and with my grandparents from Kansas. *Growing up, I wasn't* always sure who I was or where I was going.
>
> *Then, when I was about your age, I decided* to become a community organizer. *I wrote* letters to every organization in the country that I could think of. And for a while, *I got no* response. Finally, this small group of churches on the

South Side of Chicago wrote back and offered me a job to come help neighborhoods devastated by steel-plant closings. My mother and grandparents wanted me to go to law school. My friends were applying to jobs on Wall Street. *I didn't know* a soul in Chicago, and the salary was about $12,000 a year, plus $2,000 to buy an old, beat-up car.

I still remember a conversation I had with an older man before I left. He looked and said, "Barack, I'll give you a bit of advice. Forget this community organizing business and do something that's gonna make you some money. You can't change the world, and people won't appreciate you trying. You've got a nice voice. What you should do is go into television broadcasting. I'm telling you, you've got a future."

Now, he may have had a point about the TV thing. *And to tell you the truth, I didn't have* a clear answer about what I was doing. *I wanted to* step into the currents of history and help people fight for their dreams but didn't know what my role would be. *I was inspired* by what people like Harris did in the civil rights movement, but when *I got to* Chicago, there were no marches, no soaring speeches. In the shadow of an empty steel plant, there were just a lot of folks struggling. Day after day, *I heard* no a lot more than I heard yes. *I saw* plenty of empty chairs in those meetings we put together.

But even as *I discovered* that you can't bend history to your will, *I found* that you could do your part to see that, in the words of Dr. King, it "bends toward justice." In church basements and around kitchen tables, block by block, we brought the community together, registered new voters, fought for new jobs, and helped people live lives with some measure of dignity.[5] [*Emphases provided*]

As Obama employed the strong use of pronouns, such as when he commented, "when *I* was about *your* age," he made the tone of this talk very personal. Combined with light-hearted humor and informal language such as, "To tell you the truth, I didn't have a clear answer," Obama succeeded in delivering an intimate address that hit close to the heart.

⇥ PERSONALIZING THE MESSAGE: THE "WE" CONNECTION

Employing "we" has a similar effect to the "I-you" connection. It helps to send the message that the speaker and those listening are on the same team, in the same boat, facing the same fate. Consider this example from Obama's June 3, 2008 primary night speech in Minnesota:

All of *you chose* to support a candidate you believe in deeply. But at the end of the day, we aren't the reason you came out and waited in lines that stretched block after block to make your voice heard. *You didn't do* that because of me or Senator Clinton or anyone else. *You did it* because *you know* in *your hearts* that at this moment—a moment that will define a generation—*we cannot* afford to keep doing what we've been doing. *We owe* our children a better future. *We owe* our country a better future. And for all those who dream of that future tonight, *I say, let u*s begin the work together.

Let us unite in common effort to chart a new course for America.[6] [*Emphases provided*]

Similarly, Obama used references to "I-you-we" very effectively during his December 27, 2007, "Our Moment Is Now" speech:

. . . *I know* that when the American people believe in something, it happens.

If you believe, then we can tell the lobbyists that their days of setting the agenda in Washington are over.

If you believe, then we can stop making promises to America's workers and start delivering—jobs that pay, health care that's affordable, pensions you can count on, and a tax cut for working Americans instead of the companies who send their jobs overseas.

If you believe, we can offer a world-class education to every child and pay our teachers more and make college dreams a reality for every American.

If you believe, we can save this planet and end our dependence on foreign oil.

If you believe, we can end this war, close Guantanamo, restore our standing, renew our diplomacy, and once again respect the Constitution of the United States of America .

That's the future within *our reach. . . .*[7] [*Emphases provided*]

Obama's excellent ability to personalize his message has enabled him to make great strides in winning hearts and minds. For leaders aiming to sway and inspire listeners, consider how you can employ pronouns effectively—leveraging the "I," "you," "we" connection. Personalizing messages can add great power to communication.

⇥ WHAT WE'VE LEARNED— ⇤
PRACTICES FOR WINNING HEARTS AND MINDS

Obama's success demonstrates many best practices with regard to winning hearts and minds. When seeking to use communicative power to sway others, it is advisable to adapt remarks to the audience, speaking meaningfully to audience members about the issues they most care about. The skilled communicator keeps things personal by leveraging personal pronouns—"I," "you," and "we"—to connect more closely with audience members, establishing a sense of one-to-one conversation. They talk about their own experiences to give power and authority to their words, so listeners understand, "She's been there; she knows." Excellent communicators use details skillfully to demonstrate that they understand the experiences and perspectives of audience members. Empathy and action—these are things the audience seeks. A skilled communicator will use details to show that they realize, remember, and will be responsive to the needs and desires of their audiences.

CHAPTER 5

CONVEYING VISION

Barack Obama has distinguished himself as a man of vision who has dared to pursue a dream of breaking historic barriers, redefining divisions in American society, and bringing about change. But it is not enough to form a vision and to believe in it profoundly. To achieve a vision, it is necessary to communicate that vision to others in an effective and compelling manner, enabling others first to understand the vision and inspiring them ultimately to embrace it.

For years, observers have noted Barack Obama's ability to communicate his vision with great success. In 2004, Senator John Kerry observed, "Barack is an optimistic voice for America" who "knows that together we can build an America that is stronger at home and respected in the world."[1] But there have been other activists working earnestly on behalf of the poor and the middle class. There have been other aspiring leaders with extraordinary personal stories of triumph and success against the odds. There have been others also who have sought to use their leadership to bring goodwill and hope. Yet Barack Obama's success has been notably substantial—more substantial than many people would have imagined a mere forty-five years after Martin Luther King Jr.'s "I Have a Dream" speech. Why have so many people embraced Obama's vision of unity, responsive government, and change? What allows Obama to convey his vision so effectively? How does he use communication techniques as effectively as any visual aid as he conveys his vision? How does he frame his ideas in ways that have tremendous impact, particularly given the time constraints of a typical speech?

This chapter delves into the techniques that Obama employs to convey vision in ways that are lucid, relevant, and compelling. We can learn lessons from the way Obama references history and frames ideas in familiar terms. We can glean best practices from the way he employs vivid language, relies on symbolic and dynamic imagery and uses "backward loops." We can deepen our skills as we assess how he draws on the power of corollaries, personifies ideas, and provides "just enough" detail for maximum impact. Together, these communication practices have enabled Barack Obama to communicate his vision effectively, inspiring millions of listeners to embrace it.

REFERENCING HISTORY AND THE FAMILIAR

When Barack Obama articulates his vision to audiences, he employs many notable communication practices to present his ideas in ways that are clear, germane, and convincing. The way he references history serves as one of his techniques. Obama has demonstrated that when placing key ideas in a historical context, they can become more digestible because they are placed in a context that listeners understand. When Obama communicates his ideas as part of the cherished traditions with which audience members are familiar, the ideas can become perceived as a natural extension of or progression from those traditions. Consider this example, when Barack Obama articulates his vision of an America committed to addressing social issues such as homelessness, violence, living wages, health care, and education. Obama skillfully places his ideas in a historical context, referencing the iconic American leader Robert Kennedy:

> I was only seven when Bobby Kennedy died. Many of the people in this room knew him as brother, as husband, as father, as friend....
>
> [T]he idealism of Robert Kennedy—the unfinished legacy that calls us still—is a fundamental belief in the continued perfection of American ideals.
>
> It's a belief that says if this nation was truly founded on the principles of freedom and equality, it could not sit idly by while millions were shackled because of the color of their skin. That if we are to shine as a beacon of hope to the rest of the world, we must be respected not just for the might of our military, but for the reach of our ideals. That if this is a land where destiny is not determined by birth or circumstance, we have a duty to ensure that the child of a millionaire and the child of a welfare mom have the same chance in life. That if out of many, we are truly one. Then

we must not limit ourselves to the pursuit of selfish gain, but that which will help all Americans rise together. . . .

[O]ur greatness as a nation has depended on individual initiative, on a belief in the free market. But it has also depended on our sense of mutual regard for each other, the idea that everybody has a stake in the country, that we're all in it together and everybody's got a shot at opportunity.

Robert Kennedy reminded us of this. He reminds us still. He reminds us that we don't need to wait for a hurricane to know that third world living conditions in the middle of an American city make us all poorer. We don't need to wait for the 3000th death of someone else's child in Iraq to make us realize that a war without an exit strategy puts all of our families in jeopardy. We don't have to accept the diminishment of the American Dream in this country now, or ever.

It's time for us to meet the whys of today with the why nots we often quote but rarely live—to answer "why hunger" and "why homeless," "why violence" and "why despair" with "why not good jobs and living wages," "why not better health care and world class schools," "why not a country where we make possible the potential that exists in every human being?"[2]

In linking his ideas not only to history but also to a laudable historic American leader, Obama helps to substantiate his ideas as well as to make them more understandable and acceptable. He strengthens his ability to present a vision that will be embraced. Leaders seeking to convey vision effectively can learn from his successes. Are there ways in which you can reference history to make your ideas and your vision more understandable to listeners? Take time to consider how you might reference history and the familiar in ways that enhance your communication.

⇥ USING DESCRIPTIVE WORDS AS VISUAL AIDS ⇤

Another important practice that allows Barack Obama to convey his vision effectively is his excellent use of descriptive words. In many cases, speakers present their talks in settings in which they cannot, or should not, use visual aids such as overhead slides or electronic presentations. For some speakers, the lack of visual aids might be a significant handicap. But outstanding orators master the art of using well-chosen descriptive words in lieu of visual aids. They paint pictures with vivid words, focusing at key points on words that call to mind rich images. When chosen carefully, rich language can affect a listener as significantly as any visual aid: a listener will visualize ideas and themes, which become more memorable.

Several things make certain words rich in descriptive power— their precision or the specific image they call forth, for instance. Consider the difference in these two statements:

In this campaign, we won't employ harsh politicking.
vs.
What you won't hear from this campaign or this party is the kind of politics that uses religion as a wedge and patriotism as a bludgeon. (Obama, June 2008)[3]

In the latter statement, the use of the words "wedge" and "bludgeon" conjure up specific images that make a stronger impact. They are rich in descriptive power; they don't simply "tell," they "show." In creating imagery, the words help to convey vision. Similarly, compare these remarks:

You came out to support us in large numbers.

vs.

They said this country was too divided; too disillusioned to ever come together around a common purpose.

But on this January night—at this defining moment in history—you have done what the cynics said we couldn't do. You have done what the state of New Hampshire can do in five days. You have done what America can do in this New Year, 2008. In lines that stretched around schools and churches; in small towns and big cities; you came together as Democrats, Republicans, and Independents to stand up and say that we are one nation; we are one people; and our time for change has come." (Obama, January 2008)[4]

Obama's reference above to "lines that stretched around schools and churches" brings forth images of people huddled for hours, perhaps cold and uncomfortable, yet willing to endure the long lines in order to have a chance to support him. This, in turn, implies that what Obama represents, the value of his candidacy and the importance of casting a vote for him, are all worth waiting for. That is, the word choice invoking "lines of people" implies many other things in addition to what is actually said, with all implied ideas contributing positively to Obama's image. The words serve as an excellent example of well-chosen, richly descriptive words.

Obama illustrates that leaders who desire to use communication to convey vision in a compelling manner can benefit from employing words that evoke rich imagery. Words filled with descriptive power can deepen the impact of speech. Drawing on richly descriptive words can create multilayered communication that enables a speaker to make greater strides toward articulating their vision with great efficacy.

⇥ DRAWING ON SYMBOLISM ⇤

Obama is also very good at conveying vision by employing words rich with symbolism. Symbolic images often elicit emotional reactions. For example, referring to a flag draped over a coffin evokes patriotism and notions of loyalty and sacrifice to country. When Obama mentions that his grandfather was buried in a coffin draped with a flag, therefore, he connects himself to all those positive elements. This represents an excellent choice of words. The net effect: those well-chosen words enhance Obama's standing. Drawing on symbolism when it will enhance your image can be considered a best practice.

⇥ LEVERAGING COROLLARIES ⇤

A practice closely related to the excellent use of symbolism is the practice of choosing words rich in corollary meaning. Obama does this with great skill. Unlike symbolic words, a word rich in corollary meaning is not necessarily laden with patriotic or emotional meanings. Nonetheless, such a word is multidimensional in the ideas and images it evokes. The effectiveness of Obama's communication demonstrates that, in choosing key words, selecting a word that "implies 20 others" can prove worthwhile. Think about this example:

> In the year I was born, President Kennedy let out word that the torch had been passed to a new generation of Americans. He was right. It had. It was passed to his youngest brother.
>
> From the battles of the 1960s to the battles of today, he has carried that torch, lighting the way for all who share his American ideals.
>
> It's a torch he's carried as a champion for working Americans, a fierce proponent of universal health care, and a tireless advocate for giving every child in this country a quality education.
>
> It's a torch he's carried as the lion of the senate, a man whose mastery of the issues and command of the levers of government—whose determined leadership and deft political skills—are matched only by his ability to tell a good story.[5]

Obama could have referred to some other light-bearing object, rather than a "torch," as being passed on. A torch, however, has positive corollary value. It elicits images of Olympic athletes and is associated with great achievement, great heroism, and the quest for excellence. The word choice sets powerful imagery dancing in the mind. Obama shows that leaders seeking to convey vision excellently can leverage corollary meaning to provide greater impact to their words.

⇥ PERSONIFYING IDEAS AND ⇤
CONFERRING PHYSICALITY

Obama also employs the technique of personification very well. I use the term "personification" to refer to the act of giving inanimate objects or ideas human characteristics, such as emotions or actions. For example:

Every house on the street was sleeping.

The wind began to moan and the clouds wept down rain.[6]

More often than employing a personification technique, however, Obama gives ideas physicality, such as when he sees "hope" in the "light" of eyes. In doing so, Obama ties emotions or ideas to concrete images. Giving ideas physicality is a highly effective way to present ideas in ways a listener will remember. The "embodiment" gives the imagery power; the words resonate at a deeper level and listeners are more likely to remember how the imagery makes them feel. Consider this difference: suppose if Obama had simply stated, "*I know you all are hopeful; I can see this.*" Contrast the impression of those words with the impact when Obama uses words that confer physicality, as after the Iowa primary on January 3, 2008:

But we always knew that hope is not blind optimism. It's not ignoring the enormity of the task ahead or the roadblocks that stand in our path. It's not sitting on the sidelines or shirking from a fight. Hope is that thing inside us that insists, despite all evidence to the contrary, that something better awaits us if we have the courage to reach for it and to work for it and to fight for it.

Hope is what I saw in the eyes of the young woman in Cedar Rapids who works the night shift after a full day of college and still can't afford health care for a sister who's ill; a young woman who still believes that this country will give her the chance to live out her dreams.

Hope is what I heard in the voice of the New Hampshire woman who told me that she hasn't been able to breathe since her nephew left for Iraq; who still goes to bed each night praying for his safe return.

Hope is what led a band of colonists to rise up against an empire; what led the greatest of generations to free a continent and heal a nation; what led young women and young men to sit at lunch counters and brave fire hoses and march through Selma and Montgomery for freedom's cause.

Hope. Hope is what led me here today—with a father from Kenya; a mother from Kansas; and a story that could only happen in the United States of America. Hope is the bedrock of this nation, the belief that our destiny will not be written for us, but by us, by all those men and women who are not content to settle for the world as it is—who have the courage to remake the world as it should be. [*Emphases added*]

The first statement, "*I know you all are hopeful. I can see this,*" sounds unconvincing, flat, and fails to stir a listener. In contrast, Obama's elaboration on "hope" above enables the listener to visualize the notion. The listener can see hopeful eyes. The image is vivid. Similarly, when Obama ties the notion of hope to honored history, he makes the notion more memorable and enables it to resonate at a deeper level. Obama's practice of conferring physicality to ideas serves his purposes very well.

⇥ PROVIDING JUST-ENOUGH DETAIL ⇤

Another very instructive practice of Obama as he conveys vision involves his use of "just enough" detail. He has demonstrated on many occasions his ability to calibrate the amount of detail he provides in order to illustrate the depth of his knowledge about key issues. A master of using well-chosen detail, Obama also understands the value of vagueness. Consider the remarks below, through which Obama relates the Iraq War issue in terms of one specific soldier, Shamus:

> A while back, I met a young man named Shamus at the VFW Hall in East Moline, Illinois. He was a good-looking kid, six-two or six-three, clear-eyed, with an easy smile. He told me he'd joined the marines and was heading to Iraq the following week. As I listened to him explain why he'd enlisted, his absolute faith in our country and its leaders, his devotion to duty and service, I thought this young man was all any of us might hope for in a child. But then I asked myself: Are we serving Shamus as well as he was serving us? I thought of more than 900 service men and women, sons and daughters, husbands and wives, friends and neighbors, who will not be returning to their hometowns. I thought of families I had met who were struggling to get by without a loved one's full income or whose loved ones had returned with a limb missing or with nerves shattered

but who still lacked long-term health benefits because they were reservists. When we send our young men and women into harm's way, we have a solemn obligation not to fudge the numbers or shade the truth about why they're going, to care for their families while they're gone, to tend to the soldiers upon their return, and to never ever go to war without enough troops to win the war, secure the peace, and earn the respect of the world.[7]

With his choice of words, Obama paints a picture. He has met a soldier named Shamus, but he outlines only a broad image— the good looks, the clear eyes, the easy smile, his height. Nothing else. Given the lack of additional details, a fascinating thing can happen in the minds of many listeners. They fill in the gaps themselves. What ethnicity is Shamus? The only clue is his name—a name unfamiliar to many, thus many listeners will attribute no specific ethnicity at all, except for the one they see fit. With scant description, they are free to imagine Shamus as they please. In many cases, a listener will imagine Shamus to look a lot like themselves, their own ethnicity. If so, the character becomes in many ways more understandable to the listener and the example can resonate closer to home. Free to imagine, the story can connect with a broad range of listeners, helping to create a powerful and lasting impact. This is effective use of "just enough" detail.

⇥ CREATING DYNAMIC IMAGES ⇤

Dynamic images serve as another powerful tool for conveying vision effectively. By dynamic, I mean not static. Consider this example:

That is what we started here in Iowa, and that is the message we can now carry to New Hampshire and beyond: the same message we had when we were up and when we were down; the one that can change this country brick by brick, block by block, calloused hand by calloused hand—that together, ordinary people can do extraordinary things; because we are not a collection of red states and blue states, we are the United States of America; and at this moment, in this election, we are ready to believe again. Thank you, Iowa.[8]

The words "brick by brick, block by block, calloused hand by calloused hand" create moving images—dynamic rather than static. In the mind's eye, the image becomes a moving, living thing. This helps to create a sense of forward momentum. The imagery is powerful, moving, alive. It achieves great effect.

Obama's success in employing dynamic images illustrates that leaders seeking to convey vision excellently can benefit from using words that create moving images. Imagery that becomes "alive" in the mind is likely to be remembered long after a speech is complete. Dynamic words lend great impact to communication.

⇥ LEVERAGING A BACKWARD LOOP ⇤

A much more rare technique that Obama has leveraged to great effect is what I call the "backward loop." Obama's knowledge and use of this unique technique helps demonstrate how he has mastered the art of highly effective communication. Most speakers, when seeking to create a dynamic image, put forth a picture of what they hope the future will bring. Obama, however, has also discerned the power of looping back in time. Examine this excerpt:

The scripture tells us that when Joshua and the Israelites arrived at the gates of Jericho, they could not enter. The walls of the city were too steep for any one person to climb, too strong to be taken down with brute force. And so they sat for days, unable to pass on through.

But God had a plan for his people. He told them to stand together and march together around the city, and on the seventh day he told them that when they heard the sound of the ram's horn, they should speak with one voice. And at the chosen hour, when the horn sounded and a chorus of voices cried out together, the mighty walls of Jericho came tumbling down.

There are many lessons to take from this passage, just as there are many lessons to take from this day, just as there are many memories that fill the space of this church. As I was thinking about which ones we need to remember at this hour, my mind went back to the very beginning of the modern civil rights era.

Because before Memphis and the mountaintop; before the bridge in Selma and the march on Washington; before Birmingham and the beatings; the fire hoses and the loss of those four little girls; before there was King the icon and his magnificent dream, there was King the young preacher and a people who found themselves suffering under the yoke of oppression.[9] [*Emphasis added*]

This example demonstrates Obama's mastery of public speech. He skillfully uses imagery to illustrate a powerful point. Moving the motion backwards, Obama compares the launch of another significant American movement (the civil rights movement) to current-day efforts to bring positive social and political change. Obama begins with references to Memphis and Martin Luther King Jr.'s iconic "I Have a Dream" speech. The reference conjures up for many Americans images of hundreds of thousands of people marching on the Washington mall in a commendable effort to secure equality. Obama continues backward in time to Selma, and he refers to beatings and police use of water hoses against unarmed civil rights protestors. He finally rests on the image of Americans suffering amid discriminatory conditions at the very inception of the civil rights movement.

Consider how much more powerfully these remarks resonate than a more straightforward, succinct statement might have. Instead of stating, "supporters of the civil rights movement once stood like us, facing a big challenge," Obama takes listeners back in time, referencing the many accomplishments of civil rights supporters and illustrating that those protestors had once been just like his listeners, standing at the inception of a "movement." Powerfully, the backward loop asks an implied question—if they did it, why can't we? The message transmitted becomes: *they did it, so can we!* Given the focus on a very laudable movement—the civil rights movement—a listener can be inspired, motivated, stirred by the example. Obama makes his point with powerful effect.

ILLUSTRATING WITH ANECDOTES

Finally, Obama uses anecdotes as powerful tools for conveying vision. Anecdotes allow him to use brief narration to go into greater depth and illustrate points in memorable ways. Consider this example:

This union may never be perfect, but generation after generation has shown that it can always be perfected. And today, whenever I find myself feeling doubtful or cynical about this possibility, what gives me the most hope is the next generation—the young people whose attitudes and beliefs and openness to change have already made history in this election.

There is one story in particularly that I'd like to leave you with today—a story I told when I had the great honor of speaking on Dr. King's birthday at his home church, Ebenezer Baptist, in Atlanta.

There is a young, twenty-three-year-old white woman named Ashley Baia who organized for our campaign in Florence, South Carolina. She had been working to organize a mostly African American community since the beginning of this campaign, and one day she was at a roundtable discussion where everyone went around telling their story and why they were there.

And Ashley said that when she was nine years old, her mother got cancer. And because she had to miss days of work, she was let go and lost her health care. They had to file for bankruptcy, and that's when Ashley decided that she had to do something to help her mom.

She knew that food was one of their most expensive costs, and so Ashley convinced her mother that what she really liked and really wanted to eat more than anything else was mustard and relish sandwiches. Because that was the cheapest way to eat.

She did this for a year until her mom got better, and she told everyone at the roundtable that the reason she joined our campaign was so that she could help the millions of other children in the country who want and need to help their parents too.

Now Ashley might have made a different choice. Perhaps somebody told her along the way that the source of her mother's problems were blacks who were on welfare and too lazy to work or Hispanics who were coming into the country illegally. But she didn't. She sought out allies in her fight against injustice.

Anyway, Ashley finishes her story and then goes around the room and asks everyone else why they're supporting the campaign. They all have different stories and reasons. Many bring up a specific issue. And finally they come to this elderly black man who's been sitting there quietly the entire time. And Ashley asks him why he's there. And he does not bring up a specific issue. He does not say health care or the economy. He does not say education or the war. He does not say that he was there because of Barack Obama. He simply says to everyone in the room, "I am here because of Ashley."

"I'm here because of Ashley." By itself, that single moment of recognition between that young white girl and that old black man is not enough. It is not enough to give health care to the sick or jobs to the jobless, or education to our children.

But it is where we start. It is where our union grows stronger. And as so many generations have come to realize over the course of the two-hundred and twenty-one years since a band of patriots signed that document in Philadelphia that is where the perfection begins.[10]

The anecdote demonstrates in great detail the power of small changes in mindset and the choice to unite across traditional societal divisions. It conveys these points excellently by focusing on one person listeners can relate to—Ashley. Focusing the discussion in this manner, the points are well made and likely to linger with listeners.

Similarly, Obama's anecdote below is memorable while also underscoring key themes about education and social responsibility:

> I was talking with a young teacher there, and I asked her what she saw as the biggest challenge facing her students. She gave me an answer that I had never heard before. She spoke about what she called "these kids syndrome"—the tendency to explain away the shortcomings and failures of our education system by saying that "these kids can't learn" or "these kids don't want to learn" or "these kids are just too far behind." And after awhile, "these kids" become somebody else's problem.
>
> And this teacher looked at me and said, "When I hear that term, it drives me nuts. They're not 'these kids.' They're our kids. All of them."
>
> She's absolutely right. The small child in Manchester or Nashua whose parents can't find or afford a quality preschool that we know would make him more likely to stay in school and read better and succeed later in life—he is our child.
>
> The little girl in rural South Carolina or the South Side of Chicago whose school is literally falling down around

her and can't afford new textbooks and can't attract new teachers because it can't afford to pay them a decent salary—she is our child.

The teenager in suburban Boston who needs more skills and better schooling to compete for the same jobs as the teenager in Bangalore or Beijing—he is our child.

These children are our children. Their future is our future. And it's time we understood that their education is our responsibility. All of us.[11]

. . . Well I do not accept this future for America. I do not accept an America where we do nothing about six million students who are reading below their grade level—an America where sixty percent of African American fourth graders aren't even reading at the basic level.

I do not accept an America where only twenty percent of our students are prepared to take college-level classes in English, math, and science—where barely one in ten low-income students will ever graduate from college.

I do not accept an America where we do nothing about the fact that half of all teenagers are unable to understand basic fractions—where nearly nine in ten African American and Latino eighth-graders are not proficient in math. I do not accept an America where elementary school kids are only getting an average of twenty-five minutes of science each day when we know that over 80 percent of the fastest-growing jobs require a knowledge base in math and science.

This kind of America is morally unacceptable for our children. It's economically untenable for our future. And it's not who we are as a country.

We are not a "these kids" nation. We are the nation that has always understood that our future is inextricably linked to the education of our children—all of them. We are the country that has always believed in Thomas Jefferson's declaration that ". . . talent and virtue, needed in a free society, should be educated regardless of wealth or birth."

It's this belief that led America to set up the first free public schools in small New England towns. It's a promise we kept as we moved from a nation of farms to factories and created a system of public high schools so that everyone had the chance to succeed in a new economy. It's a promise we expanded after World War II, when America gave my grandfather and over two million returning heroes the chance to go to college on the GI Bill.

And when America has fallen short of this promise, when we forced Linda Brown to walk miles to a dilapidated Topeka school because of the color of her skin; it was ordinary Americans who marched and bled; who took to the streets and fought in the courts until the arrival of nine little children at a Little Rock school made real the decision that in America, separate can never be equal.

That's who we are. That's why I can stand here today. Because somebody stood up when it was hard; stood up when it was risky. Because even though my mother didn't have a lot of money, scholarships gave me the chance to go to some of the best schools in the country. And I am running for president of the United States because I want to give every American child the same chances that I had.

In this election—at this defining moment—we can decide that this century will be another American century by making an historic commitment to education. We can make a commitment that's more than just the rhetoric of a campaign, one that's more than another empty promise made by a politician looking for your vote.[12]

. . . Over the course of two centuries, we have fought and struggled and overcome to expand the promise of a good education ever further—a promise that has allowed millions to transcend the barriers of race and class and background to achieve their God-given potential.

It is now our moment to keep that promise—the promise of America—alive in the twenty-first century. It's our generation's turn to stand up and say to the little girl in Chicago or the little boy in Manchester or the millions like them all across the country that they are not "these kids." They are our kids. They do not want to let us down, and we cannot let them down either.[13]

Leaders seeking to use communication to convey vision excellently should consider whether an anecdote will allow them to crystallize a point or make a theme more memorable. Will listeners relate to the issues or key themes more readily? Carefully narrated anecdotes can enrich communication, enhancing a speaker's ability to convey their vision.

⇥ WHAT WE'VE LEARNED — ⇤
PRACTICES FOR CONVEYING VISION

Leaders have much to learn from the way Barack Obama conveys vision so effectively to audiences. Obama has shown a keen ability to convey vision in a compelling manner, which enables others to understand his vision and inspires them to ultimately embrace it. Leaders can draw on the techniques that enable Obama to do this so well.

When seeking to convey vision in a compelling manner, referencing history can make ideas more understandable and digestible. Listeners can relate to ideas more readily from a prism of shared history and cherished tradition, and may relate better with references to admired historical figures. Efforts to convey vision are more effective, also, when leaders "show, don't tell" at crucial times. That is, effective communicators will draw on vivid language at key times to paint pictures as effectively as they might with visual aids. They know to employ richly descriptive words—a torch instead of a light; a wedge; a bludgeon. They draw on symbolic language for emotional impact. They leverage the power of corollaries to bring about multilayered communication, saying one word while implying twenty others.

The practice of giving ideas physicality can also play a role in conveying vision effectively. "Embodiment" makes ideas more memorable, such as seeing "hope in the eyes." Highly skilled communicators also employ detail effectively, calibrating the ideal amount of detail they provide as they convey their vision. At times, ample detail establishes a depth of knowledge. But skillful speakers also recognize the value of vagueness, allowing listeners to imagine when appropriate with "just enough" detail.

Use of dynamic imagery represents another useful communication technique. Effective communicators find ways to make pictures move in the mind—"brick by brick, block by block, calloused hand by calloused hand." Similarly, backward loops can be powerful, as a speaker takes listeners back in time to imagine how it once was, comparing and contrasting the past with the present with great effect. Finally, effective communicators often employ anecdotes, which provide brief narration and short tales to breathe life into key themes. Together, these techniques enable leaders to use communication to convey their vision in highly compelling ways.

CHAPTER 6

DRIVING POINTS HOME

Highly effective leaders master the art of driving key messages home and achieving the designated goals of their speech—whether to inform, influence, persuade, motivate, or direct. Barack Obama has shown particular strength in his ability to share knowledge effectively, even amid the tight time constraints of a typical speech. In Chapter 5, we see how Obama employs communication practices that have enabled him to convey vision well; he knows how to articulate the "big picture." Obama is equally skilled in supporting the vision he puts forward with well-chosen details and themes that linger in the minds of listeners long after he has uttered a final word. Several practices have made Obama excellent at driving points home. There is much to learn about how he prioritizes, addresses rhetorical questions, employs effective repetition, leverages pace and tone, and communicates with slogans.

⤳ PRIORITIZING AND FOCUSING ON THEMES ⬳

Barack Obama demonstrates that when sharing knowledge, effective speakers understand and bear in mind the goal of their remarks—to influence, inform, motivate to action, or defuse controversy, for instance. Obama has developed the capacity to prioritize the points he will share. He sweeps aside low-priority issues and promotes most assertively those ideas of greatest importance, shining a light on them. As he does this, Obama draws on an impressive array of rhetorical techniques to highlight his most important points and to present them memorably, with significant impact. Below, we examine many of these techniques.

⤳ USING RHETORICAL QUESTIONS ⬳

Often Obama raises rhetorical questions as a useful technique for focusing attention on key information. Rhetorical questions—questions whose answers are considered obvious and therefore are not answered by a speaker explicitly—help to emphasize points and crystallize attention around important issues. Obama has demonstrated how to employ rhetorical questions effectively, using them to fix audience attention firmly on key issues or topics. He then proceeds to speak at greater length about his designated topics. Consider the example from Obama's 2004 keynote address:

In the end, that's what this election is about. *Do we partic-ipate in a politics of cynicism or do we participate in a politics of hope?* John Kerry calls on us to hope. John Edwards calls on us to hope. I'm not talking about blind optimism here— the almost willful ignorance that thinks unemployment will go away if we just don't think about it, or the health-care crisis will solve itself if we just ignore it. That's not what I'm talking about. I'm talking about something more substantial. It's the hope of slaves sitting around a fire singing freedom songs; the hope of immigrants setting out for distant shores; the hope of a young naval lieutenant bravely patrolling the Mekong Delta; the hope of a mill-worker's son who dares to defy the odds; the hope of a skinny kid with a funny name who believes that America has a place for him, too. Hope in the face of difficulty. Hope in the face of uncertainty. The audacity of hope! [*Emphasis added*]

After drawing attention firmly to the notion of hope, Obama proceeds to elaborate on the notion. The rhetorical question serves as a valuable device for focusing attention, laying the groundwork for delving into key themes.

⇥ EMPLOYING EFFECTIVE REPETITION ⇤

A notable hallmark of Barack Obama's communication style is his use of unique variations of repetition. Obama draws on a wide variety of repetition techniques that give power to his ora-tion—conduplicatio, anaphora, epistrophe, and mesodiplosis, among them. These rhetorical techniques help him to structure his key ideas and themes and drive key points home. Before delving into his remarks, however, let's take a look at definitions and examples.

Conduplicatio is the recurrence of a word or phrase found anywhere in one sentence or clause near the beginning of a successive clause or sentence. *Anaphora* is the recurrence of the same word, words, or phrases at the start of successive sentences, phrases, and clauses. Both are excellent tools for focusing attention on key words, and ideas, since those words or ideas are emphasized at the start of a successive sentence, phrase, or clause. Consider, for instance, these examples of anaphora:

> *To envision* the goal is good. *To envision* the execution is necessary. *To envision* the victory is crucial.

> *To give them* guidance is advisable. *To give them* motivation is required. *To give them* encouragement is imperative.

> *What does he* want? *What does he* hope for? *What does he* seek?

Repetition techniques such as anaphora have helped enhance the communicative power of many famous speeches. We find an excellent example in Dr. Martin Luther King Jr.'s famous "I Have a Dream" speech, delivered on August 28, 1963 at the Lincoln Memorial in Washington DC:

> *I have a dream* that one day this nation will rise up and live out the true meaning of its creed: "We hold these truths to be self-evident: that all men are created equal."

I have a dream that one day on the red hills of Georgia the sons of former slaves and the sons of former slaveowners will be able to sit down together at a table of brotherhood.

I have a dream that one day even the state of Mississippi, a desert state, sweltering with the heat of injustice and oppression, will be transformed into an oasis of freedom and justice.

I have a dream that my four children will one day live in a nation where they will not be judged by the color of their skin but by the content of their character.

I have a dream today.

[*Emphases added*]

Epistrophe, the recurrence of the same word, words, or phrases at the end of successive sentences, phrases, or clauses, is also highly effective in focusing attention and adding emphasis to the way ideas are communicated. Think about this example:

The idea *was flawed*. The planning *was flawed*. The execution *was flawed*.

Epistrophe is effective in part because it fixes attention on the final word or words in a sentence, phrase, or paragraph. There are many famous examples. Consider this:

When I was a child, I spake *as a child*, I understood *as a child*, I thought *as a child*: but when I became a man, I put away childish things.

—I Corinthians 13:11, King James Bible

Mesodiplosis is the recurrence of a word or phrase near the midpoint of successive clauses or sentences. Here is an example:

> We faced great obstacles, *yet we did not* give up; we felt great resistance, *yet we did not* give in; we grew weary from the long fight, *yet we did not* lie down.

Obama is famous for using variations of repetition to yield powerful oration. He draws on a full range of techniques and often extends his use of repetition to paragraphs. This gives the paragraphs parallel structure—helping him to communicate his messages with greater efficacy. We look at several excellent examples below. We begin with Obama's remarks about John McCain, delivered on the final Democratic primary night in St. Paul, Minnesota, on June 3, 2008:

> John McCain has spent a lot of time talking about trips to Iraq in the last few weeks, but *maybe if he* spent some time taking trips to the cities and towns that have been hardest hit by this economy—cities in Michigan, and Ohio, and right here in Minnesota—he'd understand the kind of change that people are looking for.
>
> *Maybe if he* went to Iowa and met the student who works the night shift after a full day of class and still can't pay the medical bills for a sister who's ill, he'd understand that she can't afford four more years of a health-care plan that only takes care of the healthy and wealthy. She needs us to pass a health-care plan that guarantees insurance to every American who wants it and brings down premiums for every family who needs it. That's the change we need.

Maybe if he went to Pennsylvania and met the man who lost his job but can't even afford the gas to drive around and look for a new one, he'd understand that we can't afford four more years of our addiction to oil from dictators. That man needs us to pass an energy policy that works with automakers to raise fuel standards and makes corporations pay for their pollution and oil companies invest their record profits in a clean energy future—an energy policy that will create millions of new jobs that pay well and can't be outsourced. That's the change we need.

And *maybe if he* spent some time in the schools of South Carolina or St. Paul or where he spoke tonight in New Orleans, he'd understand that we can't afford to leave the money behind for No Child Left Behind; that we owe it to our children to invest in early childhood education, to recruit an army of new teachers and give them better pay and more support, to finally decide that in this global economy the chance to get a college education should not be a privilege for the wealthy few, but the birthright of every American. That's the change we need in America. That's why I'm running for president.[1] [*Emphases added*]

The repetition of the words "maybe if" help to provide a high level of structure to Obama's remarks and ideas. The dismissive words also focus attention on the main themes, which aim to cast doubt in the minds of listeners about McCain's credibility and the degree to which McCain is in touch with the plight of everyday Americans. Obama uses this repetition, therefore, in a way that enhances the impression he seeks to convey.

Similarly, in the remarks below, Obama skillfully uses repetition to create a sense of common identity among the diverse members of the audience, underscoring the principles they share and adding to a sense of unity:

This is our moment. This is our time for change. Our party—the Democratic party—has always been at its best when we've led not by polls, but by principle; not by calculation, but by conviction; when we've called all Americans to a common purpose—a higher purpose.

We are the party of Jefferson, who wrote the words that we are still trying to heed—that all of us are created equal, that all of us deserve the chance to pursue our happiness.

We're the party of Jackson, who took back the White House for the people of this country.

We're the party of a man who overcame his own disability to tell us that the only thing we had to fear was fear itself; who faced down fascism and liberated a continent from tyranny.

And we're the party of a young president who asked what we could do for our country and the challenged us to do it.

That is who we are. That is the party that we need to be, and can be, if we cast off our doubts and leave behind our fears and choose the America that we know is possible. Because there is a moment in the life of every generation, if it is to make its mark on history, when its spirit has to come through, when it must choose the future over the past, when it must make its own change from the bottom up.

This is our moment. This is our message—the same message we had when we were up, and when we were down. The same message that we will carry all the way to the convention. And in seven months' time we can realize this promise; we can claim this legacy; we can choose new leadership for America. Because there is nothing we cannot do if the American people decide it is time.[2] [*Emphases added*]

Below, Obama uses repetition to stress unity, a strong image of forward action, a sense of urgency, and the importance of action on the part of the listener:

Let us begin this hard work together. *Let us* transform this nation.

Let us be the generation that reshapes our economy to compete in the digital age. *Let's* set high standards for our schools and give them the resources they need to succeed. *Let's* recruit a new army of teachers and give them better pay and more support in exchange for more accountability. *Let's* make college more affordable, and *let's* invest in scientific research, and *let's* lay down broadband lines through the heart of inner cities and rural towns all across America.

And as our economy changes, *let's be* the generation that ensures our nation's workers are sharing in our prosperity. *Let's* protect the hard-earned benefits their companies have promised. *Let's* make it possible for hardworking Americans to save for retirement. And *let's* allow our unions and their organizers to lift up this country's middle class again.

Let's be the generation that ends poverty in America. Every single person willing to work should be able to get job training that leads to a job and earn a living wage that can pay the bills and afford child care so their kids have a safe place to go when they work. *Let's* do this.

Let's be the generation that finally tackles our health-care crisis. We can control costs by focusing on prevention, by providing better treatment to the chronically ill, and using technology to cut the bureaucracy. *Let's be* the generation that says right here, right now, that we will have universal health care in America by the end of the next president's first term.

Let's be the generation that finally frees America from the tyranny of oil. We can harness homegrown, alternative fuels like ethanol and spur the production of more fuel-efficient cars. We can set up a system for capping green-house gases. We can turn this crisis of global warming into a moment of opportunity for innovation and job creation and an incentive for businesses that will serve as a model for the world. *Let's be* the generation that makes future generations proud of what we did here.

Most of all, let's be the generation that never forgets what happened on that September day and confront the terrorists with everything we've got. Politics doesn't have to divide us on this anymore—we can work together to keep our country safe. I've worked with Republican Senator Dick Lugar to pass a law that will secure and destroy some of the world's deadliest, unguarded weapons. We can work together to track terrorists down with a stronger military, we can tighten the net around their finances, and we can improve our intelligence capabilities. But let us also understand that ultimate victory against our enemies will come only by rebuilding our alliances and exporting those ideals that bring hope and opportunity to millions around the globe.[3] [*Emphases added*]

⇥ LEVERAGING PACE AND TONE ⇤

In driving points home with skill, Barack Obama also employs variations of pace and tone excellently. He draws on a full range of effective rhetorical techniques that focus the listener on his key points. A discussion of his more prominent techniques follows.

Adding Emphasis and Eloquence—Alliteration

At times, Obama uses *alliteration,* the repetition of the sounds of the initial consonants of words, to help drive key points home. In general, with alliteration the recurrence of initial consonant sounds may also be sprinkled throughout a sentence. For example:

> In *long lines* that *led* to the ballot boxes, you *demonstrated* the *depth* of your *determination.*
>
> His *policy position pleased* many.

The repetition of the starting consonant sound draws attention to those particular words and serves as a valuable technique for underscoring key words and ideas. Obama draws on alliteration as needed to emphasize words and concepts, and often to add eloquence to the beginning of his speeches. Alliteration can provide a musical beginning, which is pleasant to the ears. Consider how Obama began his 2004 Democratic National Convention keynote address:

On behalf of the great state of Illinois, crossroads of a nation, *land* of *Lincoln, let* me express my deep gratitude for the privilege of addressing this convention. [*Emphasis added*]

Similarly, when delivering his speech, "Our Moment Is Now" on December 27, 2007, Obama began with a subtle use of alliteration:

Ten months ago, I *stood* on the *steps* of the Old State Capitol in Springfield, Illinois, and began an unlikely journey to change America.

Many of Obama's most powerful speeches are sprinkled with alliteration, adding to the sense that he is an eloquent speaker. Consider his words as he announced his candidacy for the U.S. presidency in Springfield, Illinois, on February 10, 2007:

But through his *will* and his *words*, he moved a nation and helped free a people. [*Emphasis added*]

Similarly, Obama employed alliteration multiple times in his speech following his loss of the Pennsylvania primary in 2008. For example, he stated:

It was a creed written into the founding *documents* that *declared* the *destiny* of a nation. [*Emphasis added*]

Alliteration, used even subtly, can draw attention to words and enhance the eloquence of speech.

Picking Up Speed—Asyndeton

Asyndeton occurs when a speaker deliberately omits conjunctions (such as "and," "but," "or," "nor," and "for") between successive words, phrases, or clauses. The omission quickens the pace of spoken words. It also gives a sense that a list of words is only partial or is more far-reaching than the words appearing in the list. Specifically, the omission of the word "and" can imply that the given list is only partially representative, and in fact, goes on. Here is an example:

> To win, we demonstrated *vision, hard work, dedication, perseverance.*

Asyndeton can also serve to emphasize or amplify a point, when successive words seem to represent the word immediately prior in an amplified form. For example:

> We learned to *rise, stand, brace, fight.*

There are many famous examples of asyndeton, such as in Abraham Lincoln's Gettysburg Address:

> But in a larger sense, we *cannot dedicate, we cannot consecrate, we cannot hallow* this ground.

Like many great orators before him, Obama also uses asyndeton to enhance the power of his comments. In the speech in which he announced his presidential candidacy on February 10, 2007, for instance, Obama used this technique to make his words sound more emphatic:

. . . you believe we can be one people, reaching for what's possible, building that more perfect union.

Amplifying Ideas—Polysyndeton

Polysyndeton occurs when a conjunction, such as "and," is used between every word, clause, or phrase. It serves as a valuable technique for building up or amplifying a point, in part because the repetition of conjunctions stands out and hence the list of words seems to go on at greater length than normal. In the example below, for instance, the use of polysyndeton gives the impression of an arduous and extensive breadth of activity:

We brainstormed *and* planned *and* executed *and* achieved our goal.

We studied *and* shared *and* learned *and* succeeded.

This technique can be powerful when used for negations ("nor") or extended comparison ("as"):

As with the rebels, *as* with the slaves, *as* with the abolitionists, *as* with the freedom riders, we . . .

Obama uses polysyndeton with great effect. Consider these instances. In January 2008, he said:

I know this—I know this because while I may be standing here tonight, I'll never forget that my journey began on the streets of Chicago doing what so many of you have done for this campaign and all the campaigns here in Iowa—

organizing and working and fighting to make people's lives just a little bit better.[4] [*Emphasis added*]

In the same speech, he asserted:

This was the moment when we finally beat back the politics of *fear and doubt and cynicism*. . .

Driving Points Home with the Power of Three

When seeking to drive points home and paint clear pictures, Obama sometimes uses three words, three phrases, or even three parallel paragraphs, to underscore his points. These practices are variations of "tricolon." I will refer to them here as "triadic extension." For example, on the night of his Iowa Caucus win, Obama stated:

I know how hard it is. It comes with *little sleep*, *little pay*, and *a lot of sacrifice*.

In an example from Obama's announcement for president, in Springfield, Illinois, on February 10, 2007, he stated:

It will take *your time*, *your energy*, and *your advice* to push us forward when we're doing right, and to let us know when we're not. This campaign has to be about *reclaiming* the meaning of citizenship, *restoring* our sense of common purpose, and *realizing* that few obstacles can withstand the power of millions of voices calling for change. [*Emphasis added*]

In the preceding example, triadic phrases help to provide structure to thoughts. They also help to underscore the breadth of what must be achieved: *reclaiming, restoring, realizing.*

Triadic extensions can also be used to paint a picture more fully and to add eloquence to delivery. Speaking of President Abraham Lincoln during his announcement for president in February 2007, Obama used a loose variation of triadic extension:

> *He tells us that* there is power in words.
>
> *He tells us that* there is power in conviction.
>
> That beneath all the differences of race and region, faith and station, we are one people.
>
> *He tells us that* there is power in hope. [*Emphasis added*]

Using Triadic Extensions for Forward Momentum

There are other, more specific uses of triadic phrases. Obama sometimes uses triadic extension to establish a sense of a continuum or a movement forward. This helps amplify his points. For example, in his announcement for president on February 10, 2007, he said:

> *In the face of tyranny*, a band of patriots brought an empire to its knees. *In the face of secession*, we unified a nation and set the captives free. *In the face of Depression*, we put people back to work and lifted millions out of poverty. [*Emphasis added*]

Using Triadic Extensions to Reiterate Key Aspects

Triadic extensions are also useful for emphasizing important aspects or traits about the subject under discussion. To do this, the three words of the triadic extension should represent a succession of synonymous words that underscore similar ideas. Referred to generally as *scesis onomaton,* when used in a triadic extension it helps drive points home. For example:

> She displayed *enthusiasm,* demonstrated *fervor,* exuded *passion.*

In his remarks in Des Moines, Iowa, on December 27, 2007, Obama stated:

> In the end, the argument we are having between the candidates in the last seven days is not just about the meaning of change. It's about the meaning of hope. Some of my opponents appear scornful of the word; they think it speaks of *naïveté, passivity, and wishful thinking.*[5] [*Emphasis added*]

During his remarks following his win in the Iowa caucus on January 3, 2008, Obama said:

> You said the time has come to move beyond *the bitterness and pettiness and anger* that's consumed Washington; to end the political strategy that's been all about division and instead make it about addition; to build a coalition for change that stretches through red states and blue states. [*Emphasis added*]

In this example from his announcement for president on February 10, 2007, Obama combines triadic extensions with *scesis onomaton* to elaborate on one idea, reiterated in three slightly varying ways. This amplifies the point he is making, causing it stand out:

> That's what Abraham Lincoln understood. *He had his doubts. He had his defeats. He had his setbacks.* But through his will and his words, he moved a nation and helped free a people.

Using Triadic Extensions for a Multiplier Effect

To add a multiplier effect, Obama sometimes also employs extra conjunctions such as "and" along with triadic extension. In his announcement for president on February 10, 2007, he stated:

> [A]s people have looked away in disillusionment and frustration, we know what's filled the void. *The cynics,* and *the lobbyists,* and the *special interests* who've turned our government into a game only they can afford to play. [*Emphasis added*]

Using Triadic Extensions to Enhance the Sense of Logic

To give power to his points, Obama sometimes uses triadic words or phrases with a sequenced order. This establishes both a strong sense of logic and an amplification, underscoring a particular point of view. During his 2004 keynote address, for example, he said:

> When we send our young men and women into harm's way, we have a solemn obligation not to fudge the numbers

or shade the truth about why they're going, to care for their families while they're gone, to tend to the soldiers upon their return, and to never ever go to war without enough troops to *win the war, secure the peace,* and *earn the respect* of the world. [*Emphasis added*]

Similarly, in the same speech, he stressed:

We have real enemies in the world. These enemies must be *found,* they must be *pursued,* and they must be *defeated.* [*Emphasis added*]

Here is an example where Obama structures paragraphs using the broad concept of triadic extension, presenting his thoughts in three sets that reinforce a theme. When conveying how intimately he understands the plight of the average American, Obama mentioned in December 2007:

I've heard from seniors who were betrayed by CEOs who dumped their pensions while pocketing bonuses, and from those who still can't afford their prescriptions because Congress refused to negotiate with the drug companies for the cheapest available price.
    I've met Maytag workers who labored all their lives only to see their jobs shipped overseas; who now compete with their teenagers for $7-an-hour jobs at Wal-Mart.
    I've spoken with teachers who are working at doughnut shops after school just to make ends meet; who are still digging into their own pockets to pay for school supplies.[6]

⇥ COMMUNICATING WITH SLOGANS ⇤
AND REFRAINS

Obama also employs slogans and refrains to emphasize his key themes and takeaways. This helps focus audience attention. A *slogan* is a catchphrase or short sentence that reflects the themes a speaker wants people to remember. A *refrain*—originally a musical term, but increasingly used in the media to describe elements of public speech—can be thought of as a concise chant phrase that underscores a main idea, like a chorus emphasizes a song's theme. Obama often uses repetition as he seeks to fix the slogans or refrains in the minds of listeners. He has been so highly effective in conveying his slogans and refrains that many Americans can recite at least one with ease: *"Yes we can." "Change we can believe in." "There is something happening." "Our moment is now."*

We see a powerful example of the use of slogans when examining Obama's remarks following his primary loss in Pennsylvania. It was an important loss, because pundits questioned whether the loss signaled that Obama would fail to gain sufficient support among working class Americans. To quell any sense that he was losing momentum, Obama came out strong, conveying a slogan that enabled listeners to fix their sights on future possibilities and remain motivated. He also used alliteration to add power to his words, making them sound more eloquent and hopeful, and encouraging supporters to remain inspired:

[I]n the unlikely story that is America, there has never been anything false about hope. For when we have faced down impossible odds; when we've been told that we're not ready or that we shouldn't try or that we can't, generations of Americans have responded with a simple creed that sums up the spirit of a people.

Yes we can.

It was a creed written into the founding *documents* that *declared* the *destiny* of a nation. [*Alliteration*]

Yes we can.

It was whispered by slaves and abolitionists as they blazed a *trail toward* freedom through the darkest of nights. [*Alliteration*]

Yes we can.

It was *sung* by immigrants as they *struck* out from distant *shores* and *pioneers* who *pushed* westward against an unforgiving wilderness. [*Alliteration*]

Yes we can.

It was the call of *workers who* organized; *women who* reached for the ballot; a president who chose the moon as our new frontier; and a King who took us to the mountaintop and pointed the way to the promised land. [*Alliteration*]

Yes we can to justice and equality. *Yes we can* to opportunity and prosperity. *Yes we can* heal this nation. *Yes we can* repair this world. *Yes we can.*[7] [*Emphasis added*]

Consider another example:

The choice in this election is not between regions or religions or genders. It's not about rich versus poor; young versus old; and it is not about black versus white.

It's about the past versus the future.

It's about whether we settle for the same divisions and distractions and drama that passes for politics today, or whether we reach for a politics of common sense, and innovation—a shared sacrifice and shared prosperity.

There are those who will continue to tell us we cannot do this. That we cannot have what we long for. That we are peddling false hopes.

But here's what I know. I know that when people say we can't overcome all the big money and influence in Washington, I think of the elderly woman who sent me a contribution the other day—an envelope that had a money order for $3.01 along with a verse of scripture tucked inside. So don't tell us change isn't possible.

When I hear the cynical talk that blacks and whites and Latinos can't join together and work together, I'm reminded of the Latino brothers and sisters I organized with and stood with and fought with side by side for jobs and justice on the streets of Chicago. So don't tell us change can't happen.

When I hear that we'll never overcome the racial divide in our politics, I think about that Republican woman who used to work for Strom Thurmond, who's now devoted to educating inner-city children and who went out onto the streets of South Carolina and knocked on doors for this campaign. Don't tell me we can't change.

Yes we can change.

Yes we can heal this nation.

Yes we can seize our future.

And as we leave this state with a new wind at our backs and take this journey across the country we love with the message we've carried from the plains of Iowa to the hills of New Hampshire; from the Nevada desert to the South Carolina coast; the same message we had when we were up and when we were down—that out of many, we are one; that while we breathe, we hope; and where we are met with cynicism and doubt and those who tell us that we can't, we will respond with that timeless creed that sums up the spirit of a people in three simple words:
Yes. We. Can.[8] [*Emphases added*]

The repetition drives "yes we can" home as a key theme and slogan.

⇥ WHAT WE'VE LEARNED— ⇤
PRACTICES FOR DRIVING POINTS HOME

In this chapter, we have seen the excellent communication techniques that allow Barack Obama to drive home his points so effectively. Leaders have much to garner and apply from his successes. When constructing remarks, for example, highly effective communicators prioritize and focus well, casting aside lower priority issues and shining a light on ideas of greatest importance. They draw on a wide range of valuable rhetorical devices to promote assertively the most significant ideas and themes. Rhetorical questions help crystallize attention on key ideas. Repetition and parallel paragraph structures emphasize key points and help build to a climax. Alliteration draws attention to key words and adds a musical eloquence to speech. A choice to omit conjunctions enables skilled speakers to pick up speed, presenting emphatic words. Adding extra conjunctions amplifies points and creates a multiplier effect. When leveraging the "power of three," skilled communicators underscore key points, building momentum or enhancing a sense of logic. Communicating with slogans and refrains helps leaders emphasize themes to be remembered.

CHAPTER 7

PERSUADING

Barack Obama has delivered a striking number of momentum-building, election-winning speeches. Underlying this success is his power to persuade.

Persuasion is central to effective leadership. It is the act—or, as some would say, the "art"—of influencing someone to do something by advising, encouraging, or convincing them. Beyond informing, persuasion involves ways of conveying information that convince listeners to agree with a particular perspective. The goal is to get to "yes," a nod, or that glimmer in the eye of a listener that indicates you've achieved agreement—you've gotten through and the listener is embracing your ideas.

Persuasion plays a central role in enabling leaders to motivate and guide others to achieve designated goals. It is considered so central to effective leadership that scores of books have been written on variations of the topic—*the power of persuasion, the importance of persuasion, the craft of persuasion.*

Barack Obama's persuasive speeches have become core tools that have enabled his success. His persuasive power is evident through the 2 million individual donors he motivated to contribute to his 2008 presidential campaign. Obama's notable ability to persuade is also evidenced through the tremendous momentum he experienced in his 2008 primary campaign, his ability to fill a stadium with as many as 75,000 eager listeners, and his success in drawing a German audience of 200,000 for a single speech. What is Barack Obama doing that people find so compelling? How has his effective communication style persuaded so many people to consider his views? How does he inspire people to embrace and ultimately support his vision of the future and of change? We have much to learn from his practices—how he sequences ideas, answers nonrhetorical questions, addresses objections, uses antithesis, and crystallizes his points through juxtaposition, comparisons, and contrasts.

⇥ Eliciting a Nod ⇤

There are many dimensions to persuasion, and many types of tools can facilitate effective persuasion. Body language plays a role. Oratory delivery techniques make an impact. Voice and intonation can sway listeners, as can techniques such as employing dramatic pauses, using emphatic words, and employing effective gestures. Descriptive language paints lucid pictures and also serves the cause. In addition, Barack Obama demonstrates that other key practices aid the quest to persuade. As a master of the craft, several of Obama's additional practices are worth exploring.

⇥ Sequencing Ideas ⇤

Barack Obama illustrates that orators skilled in the art of persuasion know how to create a strong sense of logic to their ideas and remarks. The clarity of their reasoning is apparent and they demonstrate the merit of their ideas with sharp arguments.

One key to creating a strong sense of logic involves sequencing ideas. There is no "right" order, as such—only an *effective* order. The listener must be able to understand the flow of thoughts and find that this flow makes logical, compelling sense. This lays the foundation for agreement. Sequencing information should help achieve the goal of conveying ideas effectively and, if possible, help elicit a yes or a nod.

In his public remarks, Obama sequences his ideas and themes well. It is possible to observe his sequencing within concise series of sentences. For example, during his 2004 keynote address, Obama sequenced his ideas in a way that conveyed logic and strong determination:

> We have real enemies in the world. These enemies must be found. They must be pursued, and they must be defeated.

Obama also sequences ideas and themes in parallel order, paragraph by paragraph, which lends his remarks a strong sense of order and helps persuade the listener. In the following example, Obama structured his points with themes that—sequenced effectively one after the other, by paragraph—successfully reinforced his commitment to the community and ultimately helped persuade many listeners of his sincere dedication to their interests:

> *I walked away from a job* on Wall Street to bring job training to the jobless and after school programs to kids on the streets of Chicago.
>
> *I turned down the big-money* law firms to win justice for the powerless as a civil rights lawyer.
>
> *I took on the lobbyists* in Illinois and brought Democrats and Republicans together to expand health care to 150,000 people and pass the first major campaign finance reform in twenty-five years; and I did the same thing in Washington when we passed the toughest lobbying reform since Watergate. I'm the only candidate in this race who hasn't just talked about taking power away from lobbyists; I've actually done it.[1] [*Emphasis added*]

For leaders seeking to develop outstanding communication skills, a best practice is to sequence your ideas in a highly effective manner. Make sure to communicate your points so that you make "compelling sense."

⇥ ADDRESSING NONRHETORICAL QUESTIONS ⇤

Another way to enhance persuasion is by addressing nonrhetorical questions. Asking a nonrhetorical question—one you intend to answer—is a valuable way to replicate a sense of two-way conversation. The use of nonrhetorical questions, addressed at appropriate length, makes the listener feel as if the speaker is raising and addressing commonly held concerns. Referred to as *hypophora*, the practice enables speakers to act as if they are vetting key questions from the audience. A well-developed answer demonstrates depth of knowledge and aids effective knowledge sharing. Nonrhetorical questions also focus attention on key concerns and make remarks more engaging.

Barack Obama has shown great skill in employing nonrhetorical questions. Before he delivers his remarks, Obama seems to often consider: *What does the audience most want to know and learn? What will it most doubt or question?* The next task: ask and answer. Obama has demonstrated the power of asking nonrhetorical questions and providing the answers, replicating effective dialogue. Consider this example, as Obama spoke of Robert Kennedy at the Robert F. Kennedy Human Rights Award Ceremony on November 16, 2005. Obama asked:

Why is it that this man who was never president, who was our attorney general for only three years, who was New York's junior senator for just three and a half, still calls to us today? Still inspires our debate with his words, animates our politics with his ideas, and calls us to make gentle the life of a world that's too often coarse and unforgiving?

Obviously, much has to do with charisma and eloquence—that unique ability, rare for most but common among Kennedys, to sum up the hopes and dreams of the most diverse nation on Earth with a simple phrase or sentence; to inspire even the most apathetic observers of American life.

Part of it is his youth—both the time of life and the state of mind that dared us to hope that even after John was killed; even after we lost King; there would come a younger, energetic Kennedy who could make us believe again.

But beyond these qualities, there's something more.

Obama proceeded to elaborate about the relevant attributes of Kennedy. As he often does when using this technique, Obama answers the question at length to underscore his points. In asking a germane question and then answering it, Obama succeeded in creating the feel of an engaging, two-way dialogue and in advancing his key points. This technique can be applied with great success. Leaders aspiring to use their words to persuade others should seek to identify a question or two that listeners would most like to understand. Consider asking and answering a question or two as you deliver your remarks.

⇥ ADDRESSING OBJECTIONS ⇤

Obama also understands the value of addressing objections. This technique, known as *procatalepsis,* is a useful rhetorical device and an excellent persuasion tool. By airing a potential objection and responding to it, speakers can persuade listeners by providing logical reasons why key counterarguments should be dismissed. Addressing objections demonstrates awareness of key counter-arguments and provides the speaker with opportunities to illustrate why their chosen positions are more sensible. In addressing key counterarguments, a speaker can skillfully undercut those arguments, strengthening their own positions. Consider this example from December 27, 2007, when Obama addressed concerns that his emphasis on hope was naïve:

> In the end, the argument we are having between the candidates in the last seven days is not just about the meaning of change. It's about the meaning of hope. *Some of my opponents appear scornful of the word; they think it speaks of naïveté, passivity, and wishful thinking.*
>
> *But that's not what hope is.* Hope is not blind optimism. It's not ignoring the enormity of the task before us or the roadblocks that stand in our path. Yes, the lobbyists will fight us. Yes, the Republican attack dogs will go after us in the general election. Yes, the problems of poverty and climate change and failing schools will resist easy repair. I know. I've been on the streets, I've been in the courts. I've watched legislation die because the powerful held sway, and good intentions weren't fortified by political will. And I've watched a nation get mislead into war because no one had the judgment or the courage to ask the hard questions before we sent our troops to fight.
>
> But I also know this: I know that hope has been the guiding force behind the most improbable changes this country has ever made. In the face of tyranny, it's what led a band of colonists to rise up against an empire. In the face of slavery, it's what fueled the resistance of the slave and the abolitionist, and what allowed a president to chart a treacherous course to ensure that the nation would not continue half slave and half free. In the face of war and Depression, it's what led the greatest of generations to free a continent

and heal a nation. In the face of oppression, it's what led young men and women to sit at lunch counters and brave fire hoses and march through the streets of Selma and Montgomery for freedom's cause. That's the power of hope—to imagine, and then work for, what had seemed impossible before. [*Emphasis added*]

We see above that when preparing remarks with the aim of persuading, addressing objections can prove a useful exercise. For a speaker seeking to persuade, identify key counterarguments and consider whether your remarks can be enhanced by drawing attention to those counterarguments and explaining why your ideas are best.

⊰ USING JUXTAPOSITION AND ANTITHESIS— ⊱ COMPARING AND CONTRASTING

One of the hallmarks of Barack Obama's powerful oration is his outstanding use of juxtaposition. Through juxtaposition, Obama places opposing ideas side by side, allowing him to crystallize key points about the ideas or concepts by comparing or contrasting them.

When contrasting the ideas, Obama frequently uses antithesis, a technique that places two ideas side by side in a sentence or paragraph, often using balance or parallel structures. Antithesis enables a speaker to present "counter propositions," clarifying differences in ideas and contrasting opposite ideas or beliefs.

There are many examples of antithesis in famous American speeches:

[We] observe today not a victory of party, but a celebration of freedom—symbolizing an end as well as a beginning—signifying renewal as well as change.

—John F. Kennedy's inaugural address, January 20, 1961

Obama uses antithesis to great effect in his public remarks. In some instances, the comparisons are succinct—simple statements that make profound points. For example, Obama commented after the final primary night in St. Paul, Minnesota, on June 3, 2008:

We must be as careful getting out of Iraq as we were careless getting in . . .

During his remarks on the final primary night in Minnesota, he also stated:

[T]he chance to get a college education should not be a privilege for the wealthy few, but the birthright of every American. That's the change we need in America. That's why I'm running for president.

During his comments in his speech, "Our Kids, Our Future," in November 2007, Obama noted:

And so while I know hopelessness, I also know hope.

These are examples of succinct uses of antithesis that bring clarity to thought and aid persuasion. Obama is also highly skilled in using a longer antithesis/contrast structure to extend his clarification of ideas. In his remarks following his historic win of the Iowa caucus in January 2008, Obama said:

> But we always knew that hope is not blind optimism. It's not ignoring the enormity of the task ahead or the road-blocks that stand in our path. It's not sitting on the side-lines or shirking from a fight. Hope is that thing inside us that insists, despite all evidence to the contrary, that something better awaits us if we have the courage to reach for it, and to work for it, and to fight for it.

Below, Obama juxtaposes ideas in succession in order to clarify the character of the Democratic party:

> Our party—the Democratic party—has always been at its best when we've led not by polls, but by principle; not by calculation, but by conviction; when we've called all Americans to a common purpose—a higher purpose.[2]

Obama draws on many additional variations of juxtaposition/antithesis. Their net effect is to sharpen the persuasive power of his remarks. Let's delve into some of his key practices.

Juxtaposition and Tricolon

At times Obama combines juxtaposition with other rhetorical techniques such as triadic extension to bring precision to his contrast of ideas. During his announcement for president in Springfield, Illinois, on February 10, 2007, for example, he blended juxtaposition with triadic extension to compare what Americans face and what they desire:

> It's humbling, but in my heart I know you didn't come here just for me. You came here because you believe in what this country can be. In the face of war, you believe there can be peace. In the face of despair, you believe there can be hope. In the face of a politics that's shut you out, that's told you to settle, that's divided us for too long, you believe we can be one people, reaching for what's possible, building that more perfect union.

Extended Juxtaposition

One of the hallmarks of Barack Obama's effective communication is his use of creative variations of juxtaposition. At times, Obama structures whole paragraphs around opposing ideas. In this example, he presents extended juxtaposition through a series of contrasts and comparisons in back-and-forth succession:

> *We have a choice in this election.*
>
> *We can* be a party that says there's no problem with taking money from Washington lobbyists—from oil lobbyists and drug lobbyists and insurance lobbyists. *We can* pretend that they represent real Americans and look the other way when they use their money and influence to stop us from reforming health care or investing in renewable energy for yet another four years.
>
> *Or this time, we can* recognize that you can't be the champion of working Americans if you're funded by the

lobbyists who drown out their voices. *We can do* what we've done in this campaign and say that we won't take a dime of their money. We can do what I did in Illinois, and in Washington, and bring both parties together to rein in their power so we can take our government back. *It's our choice.*

We can be a party that thinks the only way to look tough on national security is to talk, and act, and vote like George Bush and John McCain. We can use fear as a tactic, and the threat of terrorism to scare up votes.

Or we can decide that real strength is asking the tough questions before we send our troops to fight. We can see the threats we face for what they are—a call to rally all Americans and all the world against the common challenges of the twenty-first century—terrorism and nuclear weapons; climate change and poverty; genocide and disease. That's what it takes to keep us safe in the world. That's the real legacy of Roosevelt and Kennedy and Truman.

We can be a party that says and does whatever it takes to win the next election. We can calculate and poll-test our positions and tell everyone exactly what they want to hear.

Or we can be the party that doesn't just focus on how to win but why we should. We can tell everyone what they need to hear about the challenges we face. We can seek to regain not just an office, but the trust of the American people that their leaders in Washington will tell them the truth. That's the choice in this election.

We can be a party of those who only think like we do and only agree with all our positions. We can continue to slice and dice this country into red states and blue states. We can exploit the divisions that exist in our country for pure political gain.

Or this time, we can build on the movement we've started in this campaign—a movement that's united Democrats, Independents, and Republicans; a movement of young and old, rich and poor; white, black, Hispanic, Asian, and Native American. Because one thing I know from traveling to forty-six states this campaign season is that we're not as divided as our politics suggests. We may have different stories and different backgrounds, but we hold common hopes for the future of this country.

In the end, this election is still our best chance to solve the problems we've been talking about for decades—as one nation; as one people. Fourteen months later, that is still what this election is about.

Millions of Americans who believe we can do better— that we must do better—have put us in a position to bring about real change. Now it's up to you, Indiana. You can decide whether we're going to travel the same worn path, or whether we chart a new course that offers real hope for the future.[3] [*Emphasis added*]

This back-and-forth comparison, aided by the parallel structures of paragraphs, brings great clarity to the comparison and contrast of ideas, increasing the potency of Obama's assertions.

Broad-Stroked Juxtaposition

Another key technique Obama employs to sharpen the persuasive power of his communication is an "idea-pivot-contrasting idea" structure for presenting contrary ideas. In this broad-stroked style of juxtaposition, Obama devotes ample space for the discussion of an initial view, usually the view with which he disagrees. Next, he provides a powerful transition sentence, indicating that a contrasting idea or view will follow. Then Obama expounds upon a contrasting position, usually the one he supports. This structure enables Obama to elaborate at length about why his position is superior to the contrary one. Consider this example:

> *It's not change when* John McCain decided to stand with George Bush ninety-five percent of the time, as he did in the senate last year.
>
> *It's not change when* he offers four more years of Bush economic policies that have failed to create well-paying jobs, or insure our workers, or help Americans afford the skyrocketing cost of college—policies that have lowered the real incomes of the average American family, widened the gap between Wall Street and Main Street, and left our children with a mountain of debt.
>
> *And it's not change when* he promises to continue a policy in Iraq that asks everything of our brave men and women in uniform and nothing of Iraqi politicians—a policy where all we look for are reasons to stay in Iraq, while we spend billions of dollars a month on a war that isn't making the American people any safer.
>
> So I'll say this—*there are many words to describe* John McCain's attempt to pass off his embrace of George Bush's policies as bipartisan and new. *But change is not one of them.*

Change is a foreign policy that doesn't begin and end with a war that should've never been authorized and never been waged. I won't stand here and pretend that there are many good options left in Iraq, but what's not an option is leaving our troops in that country for the next hundred years—especially at a time when our military is over-stretched, our nation is isolated, and nearly every other threat to America is being ignored.

We must be as careful getting out of Iraq as we were careless getting in—but start leaving we must. It's time for Iraqis to take responsibility for their future. It's time to rebuild our military and give our veterans the care they need and the benefits they deserve when they come home. It's time to refocus our efforts on al Qaeda's leadership and Afghanistan, and rally the world against the common threats of the twenty-first century—terrorism and nuclear weapons; climate change and poverty; genocide and dis-ease. That's what change is.

Change is realizing that meeting today's threats requires not just our firepower, but the power of our diplomacy—tough, direct diplomacy where the president of the United States isn't afraid to let any petty dictator know where America stands and what we stand for. We must once again have the courage and conviction to lead the free world. That is the legacy of Roosevelt and Truman and Kennedy. That's what the American people want. That's what change is.

Change is building an economy that rewards not just wealth, but the work and workers who created it. It's understanding that the struggles facing working families can't be solved by spending billions of dollars on more tax breaks for big corporations and wealthy CEOs, but by giving a the middle-class a tax break, and investing in our crumbling infrastructure, and transforming how we use energy, and improving our schools, and renewing our commitment to science and innovation. It's understanding that fiscal responsibility and shared prosperity can go hand in hand, as they did when Bill Clinton was president.[4] [*Emphasis added*]

The use of broad-stroked juxtaposition and parallel structures makes Obama's remarks excellent in their capacity to contrast positions and strengthens their persuasive power. Consider another example from Obama's remarks titled, "A More Perfect Union," delivered in Philadelphia in March 2008:

For we have a choice in this country. *We can* accept a politics that breeds division and conflict and cynicism. *We can* tackle race only as spectacle—as we did in the OJ trial—or in the wake of tragedy, as we did in the aftermath of Katrina—or as fodder for the nightly news. *We can* play Reverend Wright's sermons on every channel, every day, and talk about them from now until the election, and make the only question in this campaign whether or not the American people think that I somehow believe or sympathize with his most offensive words. We can pounce on some gaffe by a Hillary supporter as evidence that she's playing the race card, or we can speculate on whether white men will all flock to John McCain in the general election regardless of his policies.

We can do that.

But if we do, I can tell you that in the next election, we'll be talking about some other distraction. And then another one. And then another one. And nothing will change.

That is one option. Or, at this moment, in this election, we can come together and say, "Not this time." *This time* we want to talk about the crumbling schools that are stealing the future of black children and white children and Asian children and Hispanic children and Native American children. *This time* we want to reject the cynicism that tells us that these kids can't learn; that those kids who don't look like us are somebody else's problem. The children of America are not those kids, they are our kids, and we will not let them fall behind in a twenty-first century economy. Not this time.

This time we want to talk about how the lines in the emergency room are filled with whites and blacks and Hispanics who do not have health care; who don't have the power on their own to overcome the special interests in Washington, but who can take them on if we do it together.

This time we want to talk about the shuttered mills that once provided a decent life for men and women of every race, and the homes for sale that once belonged to Americans from every religion, every region, every walk of life. This time we want to talk about the fact that the real problem is not that someone who doesn't look like you might take your job; it's that the corporation you work for will ship it overseas for nothing more than a profit.

This time we want to talk about the men and women of every color and creed who serve together, and fight together, and bleed together under the same proud flag. We want to talk about how to bring them home from a war that never should've been authorized and never should've been waged, and we want to talk about how we'll show our patriotism by caring for them and their families and giving them the benefits they have earned.

I would not be running for president if I didn't believe with all my heart that this is what the vast majority of Americans want for this country. [*Emphasis added*]

In the example that follows, Obama's outstanding use of parallel structure reinforces his use of juxtaposition and paints a clear contrast between his assertions of what John McCain believes and what he believes:

John McCain is an American hero and a worthy opponent, but he's proven time and time again that he just doesn't understand this. It took him three tries in seven days just to figure out that the home foreclosure crisis was an actual problem. He's had a front-row seat to the last eight years of disastrous policies that have widened the income gap and saddled our children with debt, and now *he's promising* four more years of the very same thing.

He's promising to make permanent the Bush tax breaks for the wealthiest few who didn't need them and didn't ask for them—tax breaks that are so irresponsible that John McCain himself once said they offended his conscience.

He's promising four more years of trade deals that don't have a single safeguard for American workers—that don't help American workers compete and win in a global economy.

He's promising four more years of an administration that will push for the privatization of Social Security—a plan that would gamble away people's retirement on the stock market; a plan that was already rejected by Democrats and Republicans under George Bush.

He's promising four more years of policies that won't guarantee health insurance for working Americans, that won't bring down the rising cost of college tuition, that won't do a thing for the Americans who are living in those communities where the jobs have left and the factories have shut their doors.

And yet, despite all this, the other side is still betting that the American people won't notice that John McCain is running for George Bush's third term. They think that they'll forget about all that's happened in the last eight years, that they'll be tricked into believing that it's either me or our party is the one that's out of touch with what's going on in their lives.

Well I'm making a different bet. I'm betting on the American people.

The men and women I've met in small towns and big cities across this country see this election as a defining moment in our history. They understand what's at stake here because they're living it every day. And they are tired of being distracted by fake controversies. They are fed up with politicians trying to divide us for their own political gain. And I believe they'll see through the tactics that are used every year, in every election, to appeal to our fears, or our biases, or our differences—because they've never wanted or needed change as badly as they do now.

The people I've met during this campaign know that government cannot solve all of our problems, and they don't expect it to. They don't want our tax dollars wasted on programs that don't work or perks for special interests who don't work for us. They understand that we cannot stop every job from going overseas or build a wall around our economy, and they know that we shouldn't.

But *they believe* it's finally time that we make health care affordable and available for every single American; that we bring down costs for workers and for businesses; that we cut premiums and stop insurance companies from denying people care or coverage who need it most.

They believe it's time we provided real relief to the victims of this housing crisis; that we help families refinance their mortgage so they can stay in their homes; that we start giving tax relief to the people who actually need it— middle-class families, and seniors, and struggling home-owners.

They believe that we can and should make the global economy work for working Americans; that we might not be able to stop every job from going overseas, but we certainly can stop giving tax breaks to companies who send them there and start giving tax breaks to companies who create good jobs right here in America. We can invest in the types of renewable energy that won't just reduce our dependence on oil and save our planet, but create up to five million new jobs that can't be outsourced.

They believe we can train our workers for those new jobs and keep the most productive workforce the most competitive workforce in the world if we fix our public education system by investing in what works and finding out what doesn't; if we invest in early childhood education and finally make college affordable for everyone who wants to go; if we stop talking about how great our teachers are and start rewarding them for their greatness.

They believe that if you work your entire life, you deserve to retire with dignity and respect, which means a pension you can count on, and Social Security that's always there.

This is what the people I've met believe about the country they love. It doesn't matter if they're Democrats or Republicans; whether they're from the smallest towns or the biggest cities; whether they hunt or they don't; whether they go to church, or temple, or mosque, or not. We may come from different places and have different stories, but we share common hopes and one very American dream.

That is the dream I am running to help restore in this election. If I get the chance, that is what I'll be talking about from now until November. That is the choice that I'll offer the American people—four more years of what we had for the last eight or fundamental change in Washington. [*Emphasis added*]

Finally, in this additional example, Obama draws on the experience of Martin Luther King Jr. He uses juxtaposition to crystallize his ideas in ways that might provide them greater influence:

> [I]f Dr. King could love his jailor; if he could call on the faithful who once sat where you do to forgive those who set dogs and fire hoses upon them, then surely we can look past what divides us in our time, and bind up our wounds, and erase the empathy deficit that exists in our hearts.
>
> But if changing our hearts and minds is the first critical step, we cannot stop there. *It is not enough* to bemoan the plight of poor children in this country and remain unwilling to push our elected officials to provide the resources to fix our schools. *It is not enough* to decry the disparities of health care and yet allow the insurance companies and the drug companies to block much needed reforms. *It is not enough* for us to abhor the costs of a misguided war, and yet allow ourselves to be driven by a politics of fear that sees the threat of attack as way to scare up votes instead of a call to come together around a common effort.
>
> *The scripture tells us that we are judged not just by word, but by deed.* And if we are to truly bring about the unity that is so crucial in this time, *we must* find it within ourselves to act on what we know; to understand that living up to this country's ideals and its possibilities will require great effort and resources; sacrifice and stamina.
>
> And that is what is at stake in the great political debate we are having today. The changes that are needed are not just a matter of tinkering at the edges, and they will not come if politicians simply tell us what we want to hear.

All of us will be called upon to make some sacrifice. None of us will be exempt from responsibility. *We will have* to fight to fix our schools, but *we will also* have to challenge ourselves to be better parents. We will have to confront the biases in our criminal justice system, but *we will also have* to acknowledge the deep-seated violence that still resides in our own communities and marshal the will to break its grip.

That is how we will bring about the change we seek. *That is how* Dr. King led this country through the wilderness. He did it with words—words that he spoke not just to the children of slaves, but the children of slave owners. Words that inspired not just black but also white; not just the Christian but the Jew; not just the Southerner but also the Northerner.

He led with words, but he also led with deeds. He also led by example. *He led by* marching and going to jail and suffering threats and being away from his family. *He led by* taking a stand against a war, knowing full well that it would diminish his popularity. *He led by* challenging our economic structures, understanding that it would cause discomfort. Dr. King understood that unity cannot be won on the cheap; that we would have to earn it through great effort and determination.[5] [*Emphases provided*]

Obama's varied uses of juxtaposition and comparison/contrast offer many best practices. For leaders seeking to use communication to persuade others, consider the many variations of juxtaposition, comparing, and contrasting. Draw on these useful techniques when they will help you crystallize your arguments, clarify your points, or draw attention to why your positions or ideas are worth adopting.

⇥ WHAT WE'VE LEARNED— ⇤
PRACTICES FOR PERSUADING

In this chapter, we have seen the valuable communication techniques that allow Barack Obama to persuade others so effectively. Obama has mastered an ability to persuade others, eliciting a nod, a glimmer in the eye, the "yes." Leaders can glean many lessons from his successful techniques. When constructing remarks, for example, sequencing ideas can be useful— within a single sentence, among multiple sentences, even among paragraphs. Sequencing helps provide a strong sense of logic to remarks, crystallizing the clarity of reasoning so that speakers seem to make "compelling sense." Addressing nonrhetorical questions is also a useful practice. This helps communicators replicate two-way conversation, as if they are vetting questions. Excellent communicators will often identify questions the audience would most like to probe. Then, they ask and answer. Well-developed answers impress listeners and enhance effective knowledge sharing.

Addressing key objections is also a valuable persuasion technique. In addressing objections, the skilled communicator demonstrates awareness of key counterarguments and undercuts those counterarguments, showing why their position is superior. In the quest to persuade, comparison and contrast can also play a role. Leaders can clarify key points by placing ideas side-by-side for comparison and contrast within a single sentence, among multiple sentences or among paragraphs. A skilled communicator will draw as needed on a wide variety of techniques—whether presenting comparison with a back-and-forth succession or with an "idea-pivot-contrasting idea" construction. In their many variations, comparison and contrast, juxtaposition and antithesis give remarks greater potency, as excellent communicators sharpen the differences between their ideas and opposing views, in order to persuade listeners that their ideas are best.

CHAPTER 8

FACING AND OVERCOMING CONTROVERSY

M ost leaders face controversy at some point in their careers. A slip of the tongue. An unintended slight. A miscommunication. A surrogate misspeaking. These and other circumstances can all give rise to difficult situations. Barack Obama has demonstrated a notable ability to survive controversy and thrive in the aftermath. He illustrates that, often times, how you respond to controversy is more important than the controversy itself. Various controversies have derailed other shining political careers—Gary Hart's affair, Gerald Ford's pardon of Richard Nixon, public doubts arising after "swiftboat" attacks on John Kerry. Barack Obama has faced his share as well—his association with Reverend Jeremiah Wright, who uttered incendiary comments that undercut Obama's messages of unity; the unsolicited endorsement of Minister Louis Farrakhan; and Obama's own poorly worded remarks about middle Americans clinging to guns and religion. How has Barack Obama successfully used strong communication skills to weather these storms and thrive in their wake, with his reputation largely in tact and his brand scarcely tarnished?

There are valuable lessons to be learned from how Obama addresses and overcomes controversy. He skillfully resets the tone of the conversation as he employs gracious beginnings, focuses on his goals, exudes humility and leverages props. His ability to address controversy head-on, accepting responsibility when appropriate, has helped bring relatively quick resolutions. His skill in standing strong in his beliefs and continuing to deliver tough messages, even in the wake of controversy, has also enabled him to thrive. Let's delve into these communication practices that have aided Obama's ability to face and overcome controversy.

⇥ KNOWING YOUR GOALS: ⇤
REJECTING *and* DENOUNCING

When addressing controversy, it helps to clearly identify your goals. This can guide subsequent choices—how humbly you should act, your ideal body language, the props you might gather around you or the venue where you might offer your apology. When considered with care, these factors can work together to help yield good resolutions. Barack Obama has shown considerable skill in identifying his goals before he addresses controversy in public settings. A good example occurred when he addressed, during a presidential debate with Senator Hillary

Clinton, an issue regarding Nation of Islam leader Louis Farrakhan. Days before the debate, Farrakhan backed Obama's candidacy at a national convention. During the February 26, 2008 presidential debate, moderator Tim Russert asked Obama, "Do you accept the support of Louis Farrakhan?"

Aware of the endorsement, Obama tried to defuse any controversy arising from the unsolicited support. He replied:

> I have been very clear in my denunciation of Minister Farrakhan's anti-Semitic comments, I think they are unacceptable and reprehensible. I did not solicit this support. He expressed pride in an African American who seems to be bringing the country together. I obviously can't censor him. But it is not support that I sought, and we're not doing anything, I assure you, formally or informally with Mr. Farrakhan. . . .
>
> Tim, I have some of the strongest support from the Jewish community in my hometown of Chicago and in this presidential campaign. And the reason is because I have been a stalwart friend of Israel's. I think they are one of our most important allies in the region, and I think that their security is sacrosanct and that the United States is in a special relationship with them, as is true with my relationship with the Jewish community.
>
> And the reason that I have such strong support is because they know that not only would I not tolerate anti-Semitism in any form, but also because of the fact that what I want to do is rebuild what I consider to be a historic relationship between the African American community and the Jewish community.

You know, I would not be sitting here were it not for a whole host of Jewish Americans, who supported the civil rights movement and helped to ensure that justice was served in the South. And that coalition has frayed over time around a whole host of issues, and part of my task in this process is making sure that those lines of communication and understanding are reopened.

However, seizing on the fact that Obama did not use the term "reject" in his repudiation of Farrakhan, Senator Hillary Clinton said:

I just want to add something here, because I faced a similar situation when I ran for the senate in 2000 in New York. . . . The Independence Party was under the control of people who were anti-Semitic, anti-Israel. And I made it very clear that I did not want their support. I rejected it. . . . I was willing to take that stand. . . .

When Russert asked Clinton, "Are you suggesting Senator Obama is not standing on principle?" she replied, "No. I'm just saying that you asked specifically if he would reject it. And there's a difference between denouncing and rejecting."

Obama understood that Clinton's comments had put him in a bad spot and that he could potentially emerge from the debate more deeply enveloped in controversy. Obama kept his eyes on his goals of distancing himself from Farrakhan and articulating unwavering support for Israel. He reacted quickly, without further prompting from Russert, saying:

I have to say I don't see a difference between denouncing and rejecting. There's no formal offer of help from Minister Farrakhan that would involve me rejecting it. But if the word "reject" Senator Clinton feels is stronger than the word "denounce," then I'm happy to concede the point, and I would reject and denounce.

The audience burst into applause. They recognized that Obama had just doused a potential firestorm. Keeping his eyes on his goals, Obama had spoken the right words in a firm manner and quelled a controversy that could have lingered for weeks and done considerable damage to his campaign. An important lesson: before facing controversy, be clear about your goals; while addressing the difficult situation, align your actions, words, and behavior in ways that are consistent with your goals.

⇥ RECASTING THE TONE: ⇤ HUMILITY AND GRACIOUS BEGINNINGS

Humility and graciousness have also played a role in Obama's success in weathering controversies. His success teaches many lessons. For example, from his behavior we can see that the way you initially present yourself to people as you face controversy is very important. In some ways, it is like making a first impression all over again. In light of a prevailing controversy, your character or judgment may have been placed in doubt. You need to impress people all over again. First and foremost, don't appear defiant. Additionally, bear in mind that defensiveness normally undercuts your purpose also. If possible, appear humble and gracious as you begin to address a difficult situation. "To err is to be human"—this is well accepted and people are often willing to forgive, but they are more *likely* to forgive when you convey a sense of humility or remorse.

To this end, when addressing controversy, body language plays a large role in your success. Just as with first impressions, body language communicates important messages about whether you are sorry, empathetic, defensive, or defiant. Obama has shown the importance of remorsefulness and strength. The ideal body language often involves a fine line between looking too weak with contriteness and looking unapologetic with strength. It would be counterproductive to come into a room with slouched shoulders and your head bowed—that conveys weakness. A strong back—chin up—"look them in the eye" approach is better; that conveys strength. But while appearing strong, other nonverbal language must communicate humility or remorse—the look in your eyes and your tone, for instance. Allow body language and nonverbal communication to set the tone together, taking as much care with these elements as you do when making a "first impression."

RESETTING YOUR IMAGE: LEVERAGING PROPS

Obama has also demonstrated that when addressing controversy, gathering the right props around you can help send a message that echoes your sentiments as effectively as your body language and vocal tone. Obama illustrated this very well when he delivered remarks in response to the Reverend Jeremiah Wright controversy. Large segments of the American public wished to know why Obama had associated himself with such a fiery preacher.

Obama delivered his explanation from a lectern flanked on each side by large American flags. The image conveyed patriotism and a deep respect for America. This served as a frame in which Obama offered apologetic statements and affirmed his commitment to uniting people of disparate backgrounds in an effort to attain cherished American goals. The backdrop for his comments sent submessages highly consistent with his words and helped to underscore them. When facing controversy, this should be considered a "best practice": the backdrop and props around you should reinforce your intent and words.

⇥ RECASTING THE DIALOGUE: LANGUAGE CHOICE ⇤

Taking strides to quickly recast the prevailing dialogue is also a best practice when facing difficult situations. Your aim should be to nip controversy in the bud as much as possible. If the controversy has already grown relatively large, then you should seek to take the bull by its horns.

A good example of when Obama recast the dialogue quickly occurred when he addressed the controversy surrounding his relationship with Jeremiah Wright. Given the divisive comments Wright had uttered over the prior weeks, Obama needed to address accusations that he must secretly support Wright's view, since Obama had attended Wright's church for years. Obama came out strong, drawing on patriotic sentiments as he led into his so-called "race speech." He began by quoting the Declaration of Independence: "We the people, in order to form a more perfect union."

Before uttering another word, Obama's choice of this initial quotation rooted his response firmly within American tradition and underscored his commitment to core American values. The words helped to place Obama on moral high ground and changed the tone of the conversation. Obama was able to speak from that moral high ground, rather than from a strictly defensive position about his relationship with Reverend Wright. He continued on, speaking about the intricacies of American race relations and the challenges to equality, and he clarified how deeply he disapproved of Wright's fiery comments.

⇥ ADDRESSING ERROR HEAD-ON: ⇤ ACCEPTING RESPONSIBILITY

Another lesson we can glean from Obama's communication practices is that, when addressing controversy, he usually offers an apology early on in his remarks. His apologies are usually very clear and forthright. He admits he's wrong when it's appropriate, and he takes responsibility when it's appropriate. For example, in April 2008 Obama used a poor choice of words as he referred to working-class voters in old and economically ailing Midwest industrial towns. He said that those Americans "get bitter, they cling to guns or religion or antipathy to people who aren't like them or anti-immigrant sentiment or antitrade sentiment as a way to explain their frustrations." The comments caused an uproar.

When referring to his inappropriate remarks before an AP luncheon in Washington, DC, on April 14, 2008, Obama began with a direct acknowledgment of his error:

> Good afternoon. I know I kept a lot of you guys busy this weekend with the comments I made last week. Some of you might even be a little bitter about that.

As I said yesterday, I regret some of the words I chose, partly because the way that these remarks have been interpreted have offended some people and partly because they have served as one more distraction from the critical debate that we must have in this election season.

The forthright acknowledgment was well received. Reporters and the public appeared to concur with the motto, "If you make a mistake, say so."

Restating Ethics and Delivering Tough Messages

Finally, Obama often adheres to a practice of restating his beliefs when he addresses controversies or offers an apology. He does not shy away from, but rather stands strong in his beliefs, and he has proceeded to deliver tough messages even after tenderly addressing his own errors. For example, after addressing the ill-chosen words he had used when speaking about Midwest rural voters, Obama took the opportunity to outline his true beliefs:

I'm a person of deep faith, and my religion has sustained me through a lot in my life. I even gave a speech on faith before I ever started running for president where I said that Democrats, "Make a mistake when we fail to acknowledge the power of faith in people's lives." I also represent a state with a large number of hunters and sportsmen, and I understand how important these traditions are to families in Illinois and all across America. And, contrary to what my poor word choices may have implied or my opponents have suggested, I've never believed that these traditions or people's faith has anything to do with how much money they have.

But I will never walk away from the larger point that I was trying to make. For the last several decades, people in small towns and cities and rural areas all across this country have seen globalization change the rules of the game on them. When I began my career as an organizer on the South Side of Chicago, I saw what happens when the local steel mill shuts its doors and moves overseas. You don't just lose the jobs in the mill. You start losing jobs and businesses throughout the community. The streets are emptier. The schools suffer.

I saw it during my campaign for the senate in Illinois when I'd talk to union guys who had worked at the local Maytag plant for twenty, thirty years before being laid off at fifty-five years old when it picked up and moved to Mexico; and they had no idea what they're going to do without the paycheck or the pension that they counted on. One man didn't even know if he'd be able to afford the liver transplant his son needed now that his health care was gone.

I've heard these stories almost every day during this campaign, whether it was in Iowa or Ohio or Pennsylvania. And the people I've met have also told me that every year, in every election, politicians come to their towns, and they tell them what they want to hear, and they make big promises, and then they go back to Washington when the campaign's over, and nothing changes. There's no plan to address the downside of globalization. We don't do anything about the skyrocketing cost of health care or college or those disappearing pensions. Instead of fighting to replace jobs that aren't coming back, Washington ends up fighting over the latest distraction of the week.

And after years and years and years of this, a lot of people in this country have become cynical about what government can do to improve their lives. They are angry and frustrated with their leaders for not listening to them, for not fighting for them, for not always telling them the truth. And yes, they are bitter about that. . . .

I may have made a mistake last week in the words that I chose, but the other party has made a much more damaging mistake in the failed policies they've chosen and the bankrupt philosophy they've embraced for the last three decades.

It's a philosophy that says there's no role for government in making the global economy work for working Americas, that we have to just sit back watch those factories close and those jobs disappear, that there's nothing we can do or should do about workers without health care or children in crumbling schools or families who are losing their homes, and so we should just hand out a few tax breaks and wish everyone the best of luck.[1] [*Emphasis added*]

Similarly, in March 2008, after repudiating Reverend Wright's divisive comments and clarifying that he affirmed principles of unity, not division, Obama proceeded to stand strong in his conviction that, at that time, he could not fully disown Reverend Wright. He explained at length, in what has since been called a "seminal" speech on race relations in America:

Throughout the first year of this campaign, against all predictions to the contrary, we saw how hungry the American people were for this message of unity. Despite the temptation to view my candidacy through a purely racial lens, we won commanding victories in states with some of the whitest populations in the country. In South Carolina, where the Confederate flag still flies, we built a powerful coalition of African Americans and white Americans.

This is not to say that race has not been an issue in the campaign. At various stages in the campaign, some commentators have deemed me either "too black" or "not black enough." We saw racial tensions bubble to the surface during the week before the South Carolina primary. The press has scoured every exit poll for the latest evidence of racial polarization, not just in terms of white and black, but black and brown as well.

And yet, it has only been in the last couple of weeks that the discussion of race in this campaign has taken a particularly divisive turn. . . .

I have already condemned, in unequivocal terms, the statements of Reverend Wright that have caused such controversy. For some, nagging questions remain. Did I know him to be an occasionally fierce critic of American domestic and foreign policy? Of course. Did I ever hear him make remarks that could be considered controversial while I sat in church? Yes. Did I strongly disagree with many of his political views? Absolutely—just as I'm sure many of you have heard remarks from your pastors, priests, or rabbis with which you strongly disagreed.

But the remarks that have caused this recent firestorm weren't simply controversial. They weren't simply a religious leader's effort to speak out against perceived injustice. Instead, they expressed a profoundly distorted view of this country—a view that sees white racism as endemic and that elevates what is wrong with America above all that we know is right with America; a view that sees the conflicts in the Middle East as rooted primarily in the actions of stalwart allies like Israel instead of emanating from the perverse and hateful ideologies of radical Islam.

As such, Reverend Wright's comments were not only wrong but divisive, divisive at a time when we need unity; racially charged at a time when we need to come together to solve a set of monumental problems—two wars, a terrorist threat, a falling economy, a chronic health-care crisis, and potentially devastating climate change; problems that are neither black or white or Latino or Asian, but rather problems that confront us all.

Given my background, my politics, and my professed values and ideals, there will no doubt be those for whom my statements of condemnation are not enough. Why associate myself with Reverend Wright in the first place, they may ask? Why not join another church? And I confess that if all that I knew of Reverend Wright were the snippets of those sermons that have run in an endless loop on the television and YouTube, or if Trinity United Church of Christ conformed to the caricatures being peddled by some commentators, there is no doubt that I would react in much the same way.

But the truth is, that isn't all that I know of the man. The man I met more than twenty years ago is a man who helped introduce me to my Christian faith, a man who spoke to me about our obligations to love one another; to care for the sick and lift up the poor. He is a man who served his country as a U.S. marine; who has studied and lectured at some of the finest universities and seminaries in the country, and who for over thirty years led a church that serves the community by doing God's work here on Earth—by housing the homeless, ministering to the needy, providing day care services and scholarships and prison ministries, and reaching out to those suffering from HIV/AIDS. . . .

As imperfect as [Reverend Wright] may be, he has been like family to me. He strengthened my faith, officiated my wedding, and baptized my children. Not once in my conversations with him have I heard him talk about any ethnic group in derogatory terms, or treat whites with whom he interacted with anything but courtesy and respect. He contains within him the contradictions—the good and the bad—of the community that he has served diligently for so many years.

I can no more disown him than I can disown the black community. I can no more disown him than I can my white grandmother—a woman who helped raise me, a woman who sacrificed again and again for me, a woman who loves me as much as she loves anything in this world, but a woman who once confessed her fear of black men who passed by her on the street and who on more than one occasion has uttered racial or ethnic stereotypes that made me cringe.

These people are a part of me. And they are a part of America, this country that I love. . . .

For the men and women of Reverend Wright's generation, the memories of humiliation and doubt and fear have not gone away; nor has the anger and the bitterness of those years. That anger may not get expressed in public, in front of white coworkers or white friends. But it does find voice in the barbershop or around the kitchen table. At times, that anger is exploited by politicians, to gin up votes along racial lines, or to make up for a politician's own failings.

And occasionally it finds voice in the church on Sunday morning, in the pulpit and in the pews. . . .

This is where we are right now. It's a racial stalemate we've been stuck in for years. Contrary to the claims of some of my critics, black and white, I have never been so naive as to believe that we can get beyond our racial divisions in a single election cycle, or with a single candidacy—particularly a candidacy as imperfect as my own.

But I have asserted a firm conviction—a conviction rooted in my faith in God and my faith in the American people—that working together we can move beyond some of our old racial wounds and that in fact we have no choice if we are to continue on the path of a more perfect union. [*Emphasis added*]

Obama's clarification above was quite bold. Not all listeners were pleased. On the whole, however, the public and press seemed satisfied to hear a clear denunciation of Wright's remarks and a clarification of how Obama viewed those remarks. Given Obama's forthrightness and the sincerity with which he spoke of wanting to unite Americans, the public and the press seemed largely accepting of Obama's choice to also assert that at the time he could not "disown" Wright any more than he could his own grandmother but that he hoped to help move America beyond its "old racial wounds." Obama's choice to stand strong in his convictions won the respect of many listeners.

⇥ WHAT WE'VE LEARNED— ⇤
PRACTICES FOR FACING AND
OVERCOMING OBSTACLES

Obama has demonstrated tremendous skill in facing and overcoming controversy. We have learned many lessons from the communication practices that have enabled him to weather storms and thrive in their aftermath. Notably, leaders should always remember that how they respond to controversy is as or more important than the controversy itself. They should address controversy head-on and accept responsibility when appropriate. When offering apologies, skilled communicators seek to appear remorseful but strong. Because their character and judgment may have been placed in doubt, skilled communicators realize they must make strong impressions all over again. They avoid the appearance of defiance and defensiveness; humility and graciousness characterize their words. As with first impressions, body language, image, and voice have considerable impact on the impressions made. Effective communicators identify their goals before they offer apologies or remarks, and they stay focused, making sure to articulate the words necessary to achieve their goals. Skilled communicators remember to use props and physical location to reset their image amid controversy, as well as to reinforce their key messages. They offer their apologies early on in their remarks, in a forthright manner. They also avoid appearing as if they are wavering in their commitment to admirable ethics. Instead, when offering their remarks, they communicate their strong ethics again, standing strong in their beliefs.

CHAPTER 9

MOTIVATING OTHERS TO ACTION AND LEAVING STRONG LAST IMPRESSIONS

Strong finishes are indispensable for communicating messages that impact listeners and endure in their minds. Ideally, during their remarks leaders will convey their visions and points effectively enough to successfully achieve the goal of their talk. Ideally also, when delivering closing remarks, leaders will succeed in motivating their listeners, wielding a strong impact and leaving a strong last impression. Barack Obama has shown considerable skill in ending his speeches and public remarks with great power and efficacy. Just as a strong start helps to capture attention and engage and direct a listener, an excellent end to a set of remarks leaves listeners with a positive impression that can influence their subsequent opinions, choices, and actions. With his strong concluding comments, Obama inspires listeners, helps build momentum, creates a sense of importance and urgency to future actions, and at times directs listeners toward "low-hanging fruit"—the small actions they can take immediately to help a cause. By the time Obama finishes speaking, he has built to a crescendo, and he leaves on that high. Below, we glean some lessons from the practices that have enabled Obama to end strong and that have helped inspire not just a campaign, but his "movement."

⇥ INSPIRING OTHERS TO GREAT ACHIEVEMENTS ⇤

As Obama ends his talks "strong," he often employs words that set forth great aspirations, inspiring and motivating his listeners. Several types of language fulfill this task. Sometimes the words are simply eloquent. Other times the language incorporates patriotic words, cherished principles, or biblical truths. Most of the time, the words evoke an emotional reaction. Consider this example.

It is the light of opportunity that led my father across an ocean.

It is the founding ideals that the flag draped over my grandfather's coffin stands for—it is life, and liberty, and the pursuit of happiness.

It's the simple truth I learned all those years ago when I worked in the shadows of a shuttered steel mill on the

South Side of Chicago—that in this country, justice can be won against the greatest of odds; hope can find its way back to the darkest of corners; and when we are told that we cannot bring about the change that we seek, we answer with one voice—yes we can.

So don't ever forget that this election is not about me, or any candidate. Don't ever forget that this campaign is about you—*about your hopes, about your dreams, about your struggles, about securing your portion of the American Dream.*

Don't ever forget that we have a choice in this country—that we can choose not to be divided; that we can choose not to be afraid; that we can still choose this moment to finally come together and solve the problems we've talked about all those other years in all those other elections.

This time can be different than all the rest. This time we can face down those who say our road is too long; that our climb is too steep; that we can no longer achieve the change that we seek. This is our time to answer the call that so many generations of Americans have answered before—by insisting that by hard work, and by sacrifice, the American Dream will endure. Thank you, and may God bless the United States of America.[1] [*Emphasis added*]

In another example, Obama uses language to encourage audience members to respond to a call to service, to think of things bigger than themselves, and to realize this represents a legacy from America's great past. His emphasis helps lend an "aspire to great things" feel to the ending of this speech. It helps to inspire listeners:

Through service, I found a community that embraced me, a church to belong to, citizenship that was meaningful, the direction I'd been seeking. Through service, I found that my own improbable story fit into a larger American story.

In America, each of us seeks our own dreams, but the sum of those dreams must be greater than ourselves. Because the America we inherited is the legacy of those who struggled and those who served in so many ways before us.

It's the legacy of a band of unlikely patriots who overthrew the tyranny of a king.

It's the legacy of abolitionists who stood up, and soldiers who fought for a more perfect union.

It's the legacy of those who started to teach in our schools and tend to the sick in our cities; who laid the rails and volunteered to uphold the law as America moved west.

It's the legacy of men who faced the Depression by putting on the uniform of the Civilian Conservation Corps; of women who worked on that Arsenal of Democracy and built the tanks and ships and bomber aircraft to fight fascism.

It's the legacy of those women's suffragists and freedom riders who stood up for justice; and young people who answered President Kennedy's call to go forth in a Peace Corps.

The sacrifices made by previous generations have never been easy. But America is a great nation precisely because Americans have been willing to stand up when it was hard, to serve on stages both great and small, to rise above moments of great challenge and terrible trial.[2]

⤙ CREATING A SENSE OF MOMENTUM AND URGENCY ⤚

Another practice Obama draws on as he ends his talks "strong," is the practice of drawing attention to successes and establishing a sense of momentum, in addition to creating a sense of importance and urgency to future actions. He employs language that adds to the sense that the stakes are high and that what each individual listener does can matter. Consider this excerpt, where his language establishes a sense of urgency:

> I did not run for the presidency to fulfill some long-held ambition or because I believed it was somehow owed to me. I chose to run in this election—at this moment—because of what Dr. King called "the fierce urgency of now." Because we are at a defining moment in our history. Our nation is at war. Our planet is in peril. Our health-care system is broken, our economy is out of balance, our education system fails too many of our children, and our retirement system is in tatters.
>
> At this defining moment, we cannot wait any longer for universal health care. We cannot wait to fix our schools. We cannot wait for good jobs, and living wages, and pensions we can count on. We cannot wait to halt global warming, and we cannot wait to end this war in Iraq.[3]

Consider this additional example, in which Obama draws attention to facts that demonstrate momentum:

> We can change the electoral math that's been all about division and make it about addition—about building a

coalition for change and progress that stretches through blue states and red states. That's how I won some of the reddest, most Republican counties in Illinois. That's why the polls show that I do best against the Republicans running for president—because we're attracting more support from Independents and Republicans than any other candidate. That's how we'll win in November, and that's how we'll change this country over the next four years.[4]

The example below is even more explicit in pointing to specific achievements that illustrate increasing momentum. Pointing to these specifics has the effect of persuading listeners that they can help continue the momentum and that their efforts will matter:

It has now been one year since we began this campaign for the presidency on the steps of the Old State Capitol in Springfield, Illinois—just me and 15,000 of my closest friends.

At the time, there weren't too many who imagined we'd be standing where we are today. I knew I wouldn't be Washington's favorite candidate. I knew we wouldn't get all the big donors or endorsements right off the bat. I knew I'd be the underdog in every contest from January to June. I knew it wouldn't be easy.

But then something started happening. As we met people in their living rooms and on their farms; in churches and town hall meetings, they all started telling a similar story about the state of our politics today. Whether they're young or old; black or white; Latino or Asian;

Democrat, Independent, or even Republican, the message is the same:

We are tired of being disappointed by our politics. We are tired of being let down. We're tired of hearing promises made and ten-point plans proposed in the heat of a campaign only to have nothing change when everyone goes back to Washington. Because the lobbyists just write another check. Or because politicians start worrying about how they'll win the next election instead of why they should. Or because they focus on who's up and who's down instead of who matters.

And while Washington is consumed with the same drama and division and distraction, another family puts up a "for sale" sign in the front yard. Another factory shuts its doors forever. Another mother declares bankruptcy because she cannot pay her child's medical bills.

And another soldier waves goodbye as he leaves on another tour of duty in a war that should've never been authorized and never been waged. It goes on and on and on, year after year after year.

But in this election—at this moment—Americans are standing up all across the country to say, not this time. Not this year. The stakes are too high and the challenges too great to play the same Washington game with the same Washington players and expect a different result. And today, voters from the West Coast to the Gulf Coast to the heart of America stood up to say that it is time to turn the page. We won Louisiana, and Nebraska, and the state of Washington, and I believe that we can win in Virginia on Tuesday if you're ready to stand for change.[5]

When examining the preceding excerpt, particular wording helps to make the language especially effective. When Obama says, "Then something started happening," he draws attention to change and momentum. When he refers to "living rooms," "churches," and "town hall meetings," he illustrates the breadth of the increasing support. Similarly, when he talks about support coming from young, old, black, white, Latino, Asian, Democrat, Independent, and Republican, he reinforces the notion that the support levels are broad and increasing. Pointing to his primary wins in Louisiana, Nebraska, and Washington helps to show that "things are rolling." Emphasizing the mood—"not this time"—and indicating that "the stakes are too high" helps underscore the urgency and importance of events and potential actions.

Below, we can see another valuable example where Obama builds a sense of momentum and urgency. In this example, he uses repetition skillfully to help create this sense:

A few weeks ago, no one imagined that we'd have accomplished what we did here tonight. For most of this campaign, we were far behind, and we always knew our climb would be steep.

But in record numbers, you came out and spoke up for change. And with your voices and your votes, you made it clear that at this moment—in this election—*there is something happening in America.*

There is something happening when men and women in Des Moines and Davenport; in Lebanon and Concord come out in the snows of January to wait in lines that stretch block after block because they believe in what this country can be.

There is something happening when Americans who are young in age and in spirit—who have never before participated in politics—turn out in numbers we've never seen because they know in their hearts that this time must be different.

There is something happening when people vote not just for the party they belong to but the hopes they hold in common—that whether we are rich or poor; black or white; Latino or Asian; whether we hail from Iowa or New Hampshire, Nevada or South Carolina, we are ready to take this country in a fundamentally new direction. *That is what's happening* in America right now. *Change is what's happening in America.*

You can be the new majority who can lead this nation out of a long political darkness—Democrats, Independents, and Republicans who are tired of the division and distraction that has clouded Washington; who know that we can disagree without being disagreeable; who understand that if we mobilize our voices to challenge the money and influence that's stood in our way and challenge ourselves to reach for something better, there's no problem we can't solve—no destiny we cannot fulfill.[6] [*Emphases added*]

⇥ Building to a Crescendo ⇤

In other arenas, such as in fiction writing, a good practice might be to build up to a climax and then wind down. Not so in highly effective speeches and public remarks. To end strong means to end on a high. Outstanding orators move to the peak of their comments and end there, leaving the audiences inspired, moved, motivated, and focused on a memorable thought or call to action. Obama understands the importance of building to a crescendo (the climactic point) and ending a speech on a high. Consider this example from his remarks following his loss in the 2008 Pennsylvania primary. Here, Obama ends his remarks with an anecdote describing a meeting during which an old black man indicated he was choosing to support Obama because he had been inspired by the example of a young white woman, Ashley, who was already an Obama supporter. Obama uses the anecdote to underscore the possibility of transcending traditional lines of division and uniting for change. Through this narration, as Obama ends his speech, he builds to a high point:

> By itself, that single moment of recognition between that young white girl and that old black man is not enough. It is not enough to give health care to the sick, or jobs to the jobless, or education to our children.
>
> But it is where we begin. It is why the walls in that room began to crack and shake.
>
> And if they can shake in that room, they can shake in Atlanta.
>
> And if they can shake in Atlanta, they can shake in Georgia.
>
> And if they can shake in Georgia, they can shake all across America. And if enough of our voices join together, we can bring those walls tumbling down. The walls of Jericho can finally come tumbling down. That is our hope—but only if we pray together, and work together, and march together.
>
> Brothers and sisters, we cannot walk alone.

In the struggle for peace and justice, we cannot walk alone.

In the struggle for opportunity and equality, we cannot walk alone.

In the struggle to heal this nation and repair this world, we cannot walk alone.

So I ask you to walk with me, and march with me, and join your voice with mine, and together we will sing the song that tears down the walls that divide us and lift up an America that is truly indivisible, with liberty and justice, for all. May God bless the memory of the great pastor of this church, and may God bless the United States of America.[7]

In the language above, we see how Obama moves to a climax through the cadence of the sentences and use of repetition techniques. In places, too, words or phrases are arranged in succession with the words of greater impact following those of lesser impact—this is also building to a crescendo. In the example above, we see how Obama ends with a call to action. Consider this additional example:

In our country, I have found that this cooperation happens not because we agree on everything, but because behind all the labels and false divisions and categories that define us; beyond all the petty bickering and point-scoring in Washington, Americans are a decent, generous, compassionate people, united by common challenges and common hopes. And every so often, there are moments which call on that fundamental goodness to make this country great again.

So it was for that band of patriots who declared in a Philadelphia hall the formation of a more perfect union; and for all those who gave on the fields of Gettysburg and Antietam their last full measure of devotion to save that same union.

So it was for the Greatest Generation that conquered fear itself, and liberated a continent from tyranny, and made this country home to untold opportunity and prosperity.

So it was for the workers who stood out on the picket lines; the women who shattered glass ceilings; the children who braved a Selma bridge for freedom's cause.

So it has been for every generation that faced down the greatest challenges and the most improbable odds to leave their children a world that's better, and kinder, and more just.

And so it must be for us.

America, this is our moment. This is our time. Our time to turn the page on the policies of the past. Our time to bring new energy and new ideas to the challenges we face. Our time to offer a new direction for the country we love.

The journey will be difficult. The road will be long. I face this challenge with profound humility and knowledge of my own limitations. But I also face it with limitless faith in the capacity of the American people. Because if we are willing to work for it, and fight for it, and believe in it, then I am absolutely certain that generations from now, we will be able to look back and tell our children that this was the moment when we began to provide care for the sick and good jobs to the jobless; this was the moment when the rise of the oceans began to slow and our planet began to heal; this was the moment when we ended a war and secured our nation and restored our image as the last, best hope on Earth. This was the moment—this was the time—when we came together to remake this great nation so that it may always reflect our very best selves and our highest ideals. Thank you, God bless you, and may God bless the United States of America.[8]

⇥ REPEATING TAKEAWAYS AND SLOGANS ⇤

When ending strong, Obama takes steps to restate key themes and slogans. His efficacy in doing this is evident by how widely known some of those slogans have become: *Yes we can, Change that works for you, The past versus the future, Reclaim the American Dream, Our moment is now, Change we can believe in.*

As we saw in an early chapter, introducing refrains and slogans is a valuable way to drive points home. Reiterating refrains and slogans in the closing words of a speech serves as a means of keeping themes dominant in a listener's mind long after the speech concludes. Consider the earlier example, in which Obama restates the refrain "yes we can" in order to move to a climax and end the speech on an up beat. Obama also uses alliteration in many spots, which adds to the eloquence of his final words:

We have been told we cannot do this by a chorus of cynics who will only grow louder and more dissonant in the weeks to come. We've been asked to pause for a reality check. We've been warned against offering the people of this nation false hope.

But in the unlikely story that is America, there has never been anything false about hope. For when we have faced down impossible odds; when we've been told that we're not ready, or that we shouldn't try, or that we can't, generations of Americans have responded with a simple creed that sums up the spirit of a people.

Yes we can.

It was a creed written into the founding documents that declared the destiny of a nation.

Yes we can.

It was whispered by slaves and abolitionists as they blazed a trail toward freedom through the darkest of nights.

Yes we can.

It was sung by immigrants as they struck out from distant shores and pioneers who pushed westward against an unforgiving wilderness.

Yes we can.

It was the call of workers who organized; women who reached for the ballot; a president who chose the moon as our new frontier; and a King who took us to the mountaintop and pointed the way to the Promised Land.

Yes we can to justice and equality. *Yes we can* to opportunity and prosperity. *Yes we can* heal this nation. *Yes we can* repair this world. *Yes we can.*

And so tomorrow, as we take this campaign south and west; as we learn that the struggles of the textile worker in Spartanburg are not so different than the plight of the dishwasher in Las Vegas; that the hopes of the little girl who goes to a crumbling school in Dillon are the same as the dreams of the boy who learns on the streets of LA; we will remember that there is something happening in

America; that we are not as divided as our politics suggests; that we are one people; we are one nation; and together, we will begin the next great chapter in America's story with three words that will ring from coast to coast; from sea to shining sea—*Yes. We. Can.*[9]

⇒ DIRECTING TO LOW-HANGING FRUIT ⇐

Another important practice that Obama sometimes uses as he "ends strong" is a call to action, directing audience members to "low-hanging fruit"—the small actions they can take immediately to help a cause. Sometimes the call to action is very specific; other times, it is a general call to participate. In the speech below, Obama builds to a crescendo, underscores key points, and then ends with inspiring words and a call to action:

That is why this campaign can't only be about me. It must be about us. It must be about what we can do together. This campaign must be the occasion, the vehicle, of your hopes, and your dreams. It will take your time, your energy, and your advice to push us forward when we're doing right and to let us know when we're not. This campaign has to be about reclaiming the meaning of citizenship, restoring our sense of common purpose, and realizing that few obstacles can withstand the power of millions of voices calling for change.

By ourselves, this change will not happen. Divided, we are bound to fail.

But the life of a tall, gangly, self-made Springfield lawyer tells us that a different future is possible.

He tells us that there is power in words.

He tells us that there is power in conviction, that beneath all the differences of race and region, faith and station, we are one people.

He tells us that there is power in hope.

As Lincoln organized the forces arrayed against slavery, he was heard to say: "Of strange, discordant, and even hostile elements, we gathered from the four winds, and formed and fought to battle through."

That is our purpose here today.

That's why I'm in this race.

Not just to hold an office, but to gather with you to transform a nation.

I want to win that next battle—for justice and opportunity.

I want to win that next battle—for better schools, and better jobs, and health care for all.

I want us to take up the unfinished business of perfecting our union and building a better America.

And if you will join me in this improbable quest, if you feel destiny calling, and *see as I see*, a future of endless possibility stretching before us; *if you sense, as I sense*, that the time is now to shake off our slumber, and slough off our fear, and make good on the debt we owe past and future generations, *then I'm ready to take up the cause, and march with you, and work with you. Together, starting today, let us finish the work* that needs to be done, and usher in a new birth of freedom on this Earth.[10] [*Emphasis added*]

In issuing the closing remarks above, Obama issued a challenge to generate support for future participation. This communication style has proven highly effective for Obama, as manifested by the momentum he built during the presidential campaign and the unprecedented levels of participation he secured.

⇥ PUTTING IT ALL TOGETHER TO END STRONG ⇤

Finally, we take a look at an excerpt from Obama's December 2007 speech titled, "Our Moment Is Now." It demonstrates how to blend some excellent communication techniques in order to "end strong." Here, Obama uses vivid language—"slash and burn politics." He creates a sense of unity through the repetition of "If you believe." He builds a sense of forward movement through the use of dynamic language that helps create a moving picture in the mind: "the task before us of remaking this country block by block, precinct by precinct, county by county, state by state." Obama rallies the audience with patriotic words that resonate: "keep the American dream alive"; "change the course of history." He also uses words that evoke biblical references: "hunger for," "thirst for." Obama makes certain to point out the challenges that have been faced and the achievements and momentum that have resulted: "They said we wouldn't have a chance"; "we resisted"; "I know that this time can be different." He stresses the mind shift that must take place in order to achieve success, driving this home through use of triadic phrases: "to shed our fears and our doubts and our cynicism." He offers words of affirmation while also building a sense of urgency: "Because I know that when the American people believe in something, it happens. . . . And now, in seven days, you have a chance once again to prove the cynics wrong." Obama reiterates the takeaway slogans just before he closes: "This is the moment. This is our time." He ends with a call to action, pointing to some "low-hanging fruit":

"stand with me in seven days." Let's see how he brings this all together masterfully:

> They said we wouldn't have a chance in this campaign unless we resorted to the same old negative attacks. But we resisted, even when we were written off, and ran a positive campaign that pointed out real differences and rejected the politics of slash and burn.
>
> And now, in seven days, you have a chance once again to prove the cynics wrong. In seven days, what was improbable has the chance to beat what Washington said was inevitable. And that's why in these last weeks, Washington is fighting back with everything it has—with attack ads and insults; with distractions and dishonesty; with millions of dollars from outside groups and undisclosed donors to try and block our path.
>
> We've seen this script many times before. But I know that this time can be different.
>
> Because I know that when the American people believe in something, it happens.
>
> If you believe, then we can tell the lobbyists that their days of setting the agenda in Washington are over.
>
> If you believe, then we can stop making promises to America's workers and start delivering—jobs that pay, health care that's affordable, pensions you can count on, and a tax cut for working Americans instead of the companies who send their jobs overseas.
>
> If you believe, we can offer a world-class education to every child, and pay our teachers more, and make college dreams a reality for every American.

If you believe, we can save this planet and end our dependence on foreign oil.

If you believe, we can end this war, close Guantanamo, restore our standing, renew our diplomacy, and once again respect the Constitution of the United States of America.

That's the future within our reach. That's what hope is—that thing inside us that insists, despite all evidence to the contrary, that something better is waiting for us around the corner. But only if we're willing to work for it and fight for it. To shed our fears and our doubts and our cynicism. To glory in the task before us of remaking this country block by block, precinct by precinct, county by county, state by state.

There is a moment in the life of every generation when, if we are to make our mark on history, this spirit must break through.

This is the moment.

This is our time.

And if you will stand with me in seven days, if you will stand for change so that our children have the same chance that somebody gave us; if you'll stand to keep the American dream alive for those who still hunger for opportunity and thirst for justice; if you're ready to stop settling for what the cynics tell you you must accept, and finally reach for what you know is possible, then we will win this caucus, we will win this election, we will change the course of history, and the real journey—to heal a nation and repair the world—will have truly begun.

Thank you.[11]

⇥ What We've Learned— ⇤
Practices for Motivating Others to Action and Leaving Strong Last Impressions

When seeking to use communication to deliver messages that will influence listeners and endure, several techniques prove useful. A speaker can inspire others to great achievements by employing words that resonate, including words that evoke shared values, patriotic values, cherished principles, or biblical truths. Speaking in ways that create a sense of momentum and urgency to future actions can also be important. Obama has done this repeatedly with great effect as he has pointed to successes that continued to build his momentum, noted the increasing levels of support for his campaign, and demonstrated through the details he offered that "things are rolling."

Another best practice for leaving a strong last impression is to "finish strong." Outstanding orators will build to a high point and end on that high, leaving listeners stirred, inspired, motivated, and focused on key themes. Speakers can also consider repeating takeaways or slogans in the closing minutes of their talks. This helps to keep those themes and ideas dominant in the minds of audience members. Issuing a call to action or directing listeners to "low-hanging fruit"—the small actions they can take to aid a cause—can also help increase the motivating impact of communication.

CHAPTER 10

THE SPEECHES THAT MADE HISTORY

This chapter looks at five other historic speeches: Barack Obama's acceptance of the presidential nomination at the Democratic National Convention, August 28, 2008; his Election Night Victory address, November 4, 2008; the Inaugural Address, January 20, 2009; the address to Ghana's Parliament, July 11, 2009; and the health care reform address to Congress, September 9, 2009.

⇥ 2008 NOMINATION ACCEPTANCE SPEECH ⇤

Barack Obama moves on stage with a confident gait and bright smile, stretching his arm and waving to the live Denver audience of approximately 80,000 and to millions of TV viewers. He walks with a "presidential" air, exuding authority. He claps his hands along with his audience at times, an early sign of his connection with the audience and his comfort. He moves to the lectern and stands with a commanding posture, feet planted firmly, and shoulders squared. Dressed in a formal dark suit, his tie blends the colors of blue and red stripes, sending a subtle yet significant message of unity that is underscored by an American flag pin adorning his lapel.

The physical background reinforces his image and body language, which are intended to project him as a leader. Numerous large American flags flank the podium behind him. The staging itself—adorned with large columns—evokes memories of Washington's Lincoln Memorial, the site of Martin Luther King Jr.'s 1963 "I Have a Dream" speech. Obama stands before the formal wooden lectern as applause rings on for some time, his lips pressed together in a close-mouthed smile. His expression is humble, not gratifying—a look of appreciation and seriousness-of-purpose. After a long while, the applause begins to subside. Obama takes a deep breath and the timbre of his voice resonates as he begins his historic 2008 Democratic presidential nomination acceptance address:

> Thank you! [*The applause continues on.*]
>
> Thank you, everybody. [*More applause.*]
>
> To Chairman Dean and my great friend Dick Durbin, and to all my fellow citizens of this great nation, with *profound gratitude* [*emphasis*] and *great humility* [*emphasis*], I accept your nomination for presidency of the United States. [*He amplifies his volume. The words electrify the listeners. The audience applauds and claps and waves American flags.*]
>
> Let me express my thanks to the historic slate of candidates who accompanied me on this journey [*his tone is filled with gratitude*], and especially the one who traveled the farthest, a *champion* [*emphasis*] for working Americans and an

inspiration [*emphasis*] to my daughters and yours, Hillary Rodham Clinton. [*He pinches his fingers to underscore Clinton's importance. The audience rings with applause.*]

To President Clinton, to President Bill Clinton, who made last night the case for change as only *he* can make it. [*He motions his hands widely, indicating the words are heartfelt. Applause.*] To Ted Kennedy, who embodies the spirit of service. [*Applause.*] And to the next vice president of the United States [*slight pause*], Joe Biden, I thank you. [*Enthusiastic applause.*]

I am *grateful* [*emphasis*] to finish this journey with one of the finest statesmen of our time, a man at ease with everyone [*he motions his hands wide*] from world leaders to the conductors on the Amtrak train he still takes home every night.

To the love of my life [*his eyes twinkle with emotion*], our next first lady, Michelle Obama [*pause for applause; Obama flashes a bright smile*]. And to Malia and Sasha, I love you *so much* [emphasis], and I am *so proud* [*emphasis*] of you. [*His tone is filled with adoration. Applause.*]

Four years ago [*he draws out the words*], I stood before you and told you my story, of the brief union between a young man from Kenya and a young woman from Kansas who weren't well off or well known, but shared a belief that in America their son could *achieve* whatever he put his mind to. [*He pinches his fingers; his tone is wistful.*]

It is that *promise* [*he holds the "s," drawing a little more attention to the word 'promise'*] that's always set this country apart [*he motions his hands widely, underscoring the greatness of the country*], that through hard work and sacrifice *each of* us [*he enunciates each word with extra care*] can pursue our individual dreams, but still come together [*he motions his hands together*] as one American family, to *ensure* [*emphasis; he points an index finger*] that the next generation can pursue their dreams, as well. That's why I stand here tonight. Because for 232 years [*he motions his hand widely, conveying the magnitude of time and he stresses each word: two-hundred-thirty-two*], at each moment when that promise was in jeopardy, *ordinary* [*he points his finger in the air, underscoring the word*] men and women—students and soldiers, farmers and teachers, nurses and janitors [*his voice rises and falls, conveying the breadth of people involved*]— found the courage to keep it alive.

We meet at one of those *defining moments* [*he pinches his fingers and stresses the words, sounding wistful*], a moment when our nation is at war, our economy is in turmoil, and the American promise has been threatened once more.

Tonight [*he dips his voice, adding emphasis*], more Americans are out of work and more are working harder for less. More of you have lost your homes and even more are watching your home values plummet. More of you have cars you can't afford to drive, credit cards, bills you can't afford to pay, and tuition that's beyond your reach. [*He motions his hands widely.*]

These challenges are not all of government's making. But the failure to respond [*he moves his index finger in a chastising manner*] is a direct result of a broken politics in Washington and the failed policies of George W. Bush. [*He points his finger in the air again; he amplifies his volume. Applause.*]

America! [*A challenge rings beneath his tone as he nearly sings out the name, America!*] We are better than these last eight years. We are *a better country* than this. [*A challenge rings in his tone. Applause.*]

This country is more *decent* [*emphasis*] than one where a woman in Ohio, on the brink of retirement, finds herself one illness away [*he points his index finger*] from disaster after a lifetime of hard work. We're a better country [*he motions his hands widely*] than one where a man in Indiana has to pack up the equipment that he's worked on for twenty years and watch as it's shipped off to China [*he brushes a hand dismissively to the side*], and then chokes up as he explains how he felt like a failure when he went home to tell his family the news. [*He dips his pitch low, conveying disapproval.*]

We are more *compassionate* than a government that lets veterans sleep on our streets and families *slide* into poverty . . . [*Applause.*] . . . that sits on its hands while a major American city drowns before our eyes. [*The audience applauds his disapproving reference to the crisis suffered in New Orleans.*]

Tonight [*emphasis*], I say to the people of America—to Democrats *and* Republicans *and* Independents [*his tone crests and dips to emphasize the diverse political backgrounds*] across this great land: *Enough!* [*He puts tremendous volume behind the word. Dramatic pause.*] *This moment* [*emphasis; applause*]—this moment [*slight pause; applause*], *this election* [*emphasis*] is *our chance* [*emphasis*] to keep, in the twenty-first century [*he points an index finger in the air*], the American promise alive. [*He pinches his fingers to underscore the importance.*]

Because next week, in Minnesota, the same party that brought you two terms of George Bush and Dick Cheney will ask this country for a third. [*The audience boos.*]

And we are here [*he motions both hands toward himself*]—we are here because we love this country *too much* [*emphasis*] to let the next four years look just like the last eight. [*He glides his voice subtly up and down to underscore the words, eliciting a strong audience response of support. Applause.*]

On November 4th, we must stand up and say: *Eight is enough!* [*Applause. He flashes a bright, confident smile and utters a slight chuckle. The cheers go on.*]

Now, now, let there be no doubt. The Republican nominee, John McCain, has worn the uniform of our country with bravery and distinction [*his tone is respectful and full of gratitude*], and for that we owe him our gratitude and our respect. [*He nods to affirm his point further. Applause.*]

And next week [*he points an index finger*], we'll also hear about those occasions when he's broken with his party as evidence that he can deliver the change that we need. But the record's clear: John McCain has voted with George Bush *90 percent* [*he pinches his fingers*] of the time. Senator McCain likes to talk about judgment, but, really [*his pitch rises; he wags an index finger in the air, expressing disapproval*], what does it say about your judgment when you think George Bush has been right more than 90 percent of the time? [*His tone is mocking. Applause.*] I don't know about you, but I am not ready to take a *10 percent* chance on change. [*He pinches his fingers. Applause.*]

The truth is [*he waves an index finger in the air*], on issue after issue that would make a difference in your lives—on health care, and education, and the economy [*he motions his hands wide, indicating the breadth and importance of the issues*]—Senator McCain has been anything *but* [*emphasis*] independent.

He said that our economy has made great progress under this president. He *said* [*he draws out the word, adding emphasis*] that the fundamentals of the economy are strong. And when one of his chief advisers, the man who wrote his economic plan, was talking about the anxieties that Americans are feeling, he said that we were just suffering from a *mental recession* [*he enunciates each word, his tone conveying disapproval*] and that we've become—and I quote [*he raises an index finger*]—"a nation of whiners." [*The audience boos.*]

A nation of whiners? Tell that to the proud auto workers at a Michigan plant who, after they found out it was closing, kept showing up every day and working as hard as ever, because they knew [*he points his index finger*] there were people who counted on the brakes that they made. [*His tone is indignant.*] Tell that to the military families who shoulder their burdens silently [*his voice dips*] as they watch their loved ones leave for their third, or fourth, or fifth tour of duty. *These are not whiners.* [*Emphasis*] They work *hard, and* [*emphasis*] they give back, *and* [*emphasis*] they keep going without complaint. *These* [*emphasis*] are the Americans I know. [*Applause.*]

Now, I don't believe that Senator McCain doesn't care what's going on in the lives of Americans; I just think he doesn't know. [*He quickens his cadence, as if delivering a humorous punch line. The audience rings with laughter.*]

Why else would he define middle-class as someone making under $5 million a year? [*He waves an index finger in the air.*] How else could he propose hundreds of billions [*slight mocking chuckle*] in tax breaks for big corporations and oil companies, but *not one penny* [*he stresses each word*] of tax relief to more than *100 million* Americans? [*He jabs an index finger, accusingly; emphasis*] How else could he offer a health care plan that would actually *tax* [*he pinches his fingers*] people's benefits, or an education plan that would do *nothing* [*he motions his hands wide, highlighting 'nothing'*] to help families pay for college, or a plan [*he increases his cadence, giving the sense that the list could go on and on*] that would privatize Social Security and gamble your retirement? [*The audience boos.*]

It's not because John McCain doesn't care [*his pitch dips*]; it's because John McCain doesn't get it. [*Applause.*]

For over two decades, he's subscribed to that old, discredited Republican philosophy: Give more and more to those with the most [*his pitch rises, emphasizing the point*] and hope that prosperity trickles down to everyone else. [*He dips his pitch disapprovingly.*]

In Washington, they call this the "Ownership Society," [*he pinches his fingers*] but what it really means is that you're on your own. [*He jabs his index finger in the air, as if issuing a warning. The audience laughs.*] Out of work? *Tough luck*, [*he punches the words and waves a dismissive hand that mocks the words*] you're on your own. [*His tone is mocking.*] No health care? The market will fix it. [*He waves a hand dismissively.*] You're on your own. Born into poverty? Pull yourself up by your *own* bootstraps, even if you don't have boots. You are *on* your own. [*He enunciates each word with care: on-your-own. He draws a strong audience reaction of disapproval to the idea.*]

Well [*he draws the word out*], it's time for them to *own* their failure. [*His voice is stern and chastising; he points a finger in the air.*] *It's time for us* to *change* America. [*He points a finger in the air determinedly.*] And that's why I'm running for president of the United States. [*His tone is resolute. Enthusiastic applause.*]

You see [*he draws the words out*], we Democrats have a very different measure of what constitutes *progress* [*he pinches his fingers*] in this country. We measure progress by how many people can find a job that pays the mortgage [*his tone rings with rightness*], whether you can put a little extra money away [*he pinches his fingers to underscore the point*] at the end of each month so you can someday watch your child receive her college diploma. We measure progress in the 23 million new jobs that were created when *Bill Clinton* [*he speaks a tad bit more closely into the microphone, pointing an index finger to emphasize the point*] was president [*applause*] . . . when the average American family saw its income go up $7,500 [*he motions his hand upwards*] instead of go down $2,000 [*he motions his other hand downward*], like it has under George Bush. [*Applause.*]

We measure the strength of our economy not by the number of billionaires we have or the profits of the Fortune 500, but by whether someone with a good idea can take a risk and start a new business, or whether the waitress who lives on tips [*he points an index finger*] can take a day off and look after a sick kid without losing her job—an economy that honors the dignity of work.

The fundamentals [*his hand gestures convey that 'the funda-mentals' are precious*] we use to measure economic strength are whether we are living up to that fundamental promise that has made this country great—a promise that is the only reason I am standing here tonight. [*He motions a hand gently toward his chest.*]

Because, in the faces of those young veterans who come back from Iraq and Afghanistan, I see my grandfather, who signed up after Pearl Harbor, marched in Patton's army, and was re-warded by a grateful nation with the chance to go to college on the GI Bill.

In the face of that young student, who sleeps just three hours before working the night shift, I think about my mom, who raised my sister and me on her own while she worked and earned her degree; who once turned to food stamps, but was still able to send us to the *best schools* in the country with the help of student loans and scholarships. [*Applause.*]

When I listen to another worker tell me that his factory has shut down, I remember all those men and women on the South Side of Chicago who I *stood by* [*emphasis*] and *fought for* [*emphasis*] two decades ago after the local steel plant closed.

And when I hear a woman talk about the difficulties of starting her own business or making her way in the world, I think about my grandmother, who worked her way up from the secretarial pool to middle management, despite years of being passed over for promotions because she was a woman.

She's the one who taught me about *hard work*. [*He pinches his fingers, underscoring the point.*] She's the one who put off buying a new car or a new dress for herself so that I could have a better life. [*He touches both hands to his chest, underscoring the precious nature of his grandmother's sacrifice.*] She poured everything she had into me. And although she can no longer travel, I know that she's watching tonight and that tonight is *her night* as well. [*Emphasis; enthusiastic applause.*]

Now [*he draws the word out*], I don't know what kind of lives John McCain thinks that celebrities lead [*his tone is mocking as he makes an allusion to McCain's assertions that he is a celebrity*], but this has been mine. [*Applause.*]

These [*emphasis*] are my heroes; *theirs* [*emphasis*] are the stories that shaped my life. And it is on behalf of them that I intend to win this election and keep our promise alive as president of the United States. [*He amplifies his words; his tone is determined. Applause.*]

What is that American promise? [*Pause for impact.*] It's a promise that says each of us has the freedom to make of our own lives what we will, but that we also have obligations to treat each other with *dignity* [*slight pause*] and *respect*.

It's a promise that says the market should reward *drive and innovation and generate growth* [*his cadence quickens, underscoring the importance*], but that businesses should live up to their responsibilities to create American jobs, to look out for American workers, and play by the rules of the road. [*He motions his hands to underscore the points.*]

Ours [*he draws out the word, adding emphasis*] is a promise that says government cannot solve all our problems [*his pitch dips*], but what it *should do* [*emphasis*] is that which we cannot do for ourselves [*he motions both hands toward himself*]: protect us from harm [*he holds a vertical palm in a stop sign*] and provide every child a decent education [*he motions his hands widely, signifying the importance*]; keep our water clean and our toys safe; invest in new schools, *and* new roads, *and* science, *and* technology.

Our government should work *for us* [*he stresses the words*], not against us. [*His pitch rises and falls, adding emphasis.*] It should *help us* [*he stresses the words*], not hurt us. [*His pitch rises and falls.*] It should ensure opportunity not just for those with the most money and influence, but for every American who's willing to work. [*He increases his cadence, underscoring the point.*]

That's the promise of America, the idea that we are responsible for ourselves, but that we also rise or fall as one nation, the fundamental belief that I am my brother's keeper, I am my sister's keeper. [*He slices his hand through the air, signifying the rightness of the principles.*]

That's the promise we need to keep. [*He point an index finger.*] That's the change we need right now. [*He points the index finger of his other hand. Applause.*]

So let me spell out *exactly* what that change would mean [*he pinches his fingers, as if addressing a criticism*] if I am president. [*Applause.*]

Change means a tax code that doesn't reward the lobbyists who wrote it, but the American workers and small businesses who deserve it. [*He moves a hand toward the audience. Applause.*] You know, unlike John McCain, I will *stop* [*emphasis*] giving tax breaks to companies that ship jobs overseas, and I will start giving them to companies that create good jobs right here in America. [*He points his index finger in the air. Applause.*] I'll eliminate capital gains taxes for the small businesses and start-ups that will create the *high-wage, high-tech jobs* of tomorrow. [*He cups his hand in a "C," as if placing the words in the air. Applause.*] I will—listen now [*he points his finger in the air*]—I will cut taxes [*pause*]—*cut taxes* [*emphasis*]—for 95 percent [*he jabs an index finger*] of *all* [*emphasis*] working families, because, in an economy like this [*he leans into the microphone, accentuating the point*], the last thing we should do is raise taxes on the middle class. [*He amplifies his volume. Applause.*] And for the sake of our economy, our security, and the future of our planet, I will set a clear goal [*he cuts a hand through the air*] as president: In 10 years [*he points an index finger*], we will finally [*he points the index finger of his other hand*] end our dependence on oil from the Middle East. [*Enthusiastic applause.*]

We will do this. Washington—Washington has been talking about our oil addiction for the last thirty years. And, by the way, John McCain has been there for twenty-six of them. [*His tone is mocking. Laughter rings from the audience.*] And in that time, he has said *no* [*emphasis; slight pause*] to higher fuel-efficiency standards for cars, *no* [*emphasis*] to investments in renewable energy, *no* to renewable fuels. And today, we import *triple* the amount of oil than we had on the day that Senator McCain took office.

Now [*he draws out the word*] is the time to *end* [*emphasis*] this addiction and to understand that drilling is a stop-gap measure, not a long-term solution, not even close. [*He slices a horizontal hand, palm down, through the air. Applause.*] As president [*he moves a hand toward the audience, exuding sincerity*], as president, I will tap our natural gas reserves [*he motions his hands wide, conveying the importance*], invest in clean coal technology, and find ways to safely harness nuclear power. I'll help our auto companies re-tool, so that the fuel-efficient cars of the future are built right here [*he taps an index finger as if pointing to the very ground on which he stands*] in America. [*Applause.*]

I'll make it easier for the American people to afford these new cars. [*He points an index finger in the air.*] And I'll invest *$150 billion* over the next decade in affordable, renewable sources of energy—wind power, *and* solar power, *and* the next generation of biofuels—an investment that will lead to new industries and *5 million* [*emphasis*] new jobs that pay well and can't be outsourced. [*He varies his pitch. Dramatic pause. Applause.*]

America [*he draws out the word*], *now* is not the time for small plans. *Now* [*emphasis*] is the time [*he points an index finger in the air*] to *finally* meet our *moral obligation* [*he enunciates the words with care*] to provide every child a world-class education [*he motions his hands widely*], because it will take nothing less to compete in the global economy. [*He points an index finger.*] You know, Michelle and I are only here tonight because we were given a chance at an education. And I will not settle for an America where some kids don't have that chance. [*His tone is stern. Applause.*]

I'll invest in early childhood education [*he motions his hands widely*]. I'll recruit an army of new teachers [*he stretches his arm to the side, as if reaching to pull something from far away*], *and pay* [*emphasis*] them higher salaries, *and give* [*emphasis*] them more support. [*He motions his hand widely, signifying the importance.*] And in exchange, I'll ask for higher standards and more accountability. And we will keep our promise to every young American: If you commit to serving your community or our country, we will make sure you can afford a college education. [*He varies his volume and pitch to accentuate key words. Applause.*]

Now [*slight pause*]—now is the time to finally keep the promise of affordable, accessible health care for *every single* [*emphasis*] American. [*Applause.*]

If you have health care, my plan will lower your premiums. If you *don't* [*emphasis*], you'll be able to get the same kind of coverage that members of Congress give themselves. [*Applause.*]

And [*he draws the word out*]—and as someone who watched my mother argue with insurance companies while she lay in bed [*slight pause*] dying of cancer, I will make certain those companies stop discriminating against those who are sick and need care the most. [*He amplifies his volume. His tone is indignant. Applause.*]

Now [*he draws the word out*] is the time to help families with paid sick days and better family leave, because nobody in America [*he slices his hand through the air*] should have to choose between keeping their job and caring for a sick child or an ailing parent.

Now [*emphasis*] is the time to change our bankruptcy laws, so that your pensions are protected ahead of CEO bonuses, and the time to protect Social Security for future generations.

And now [*emphasis*] is the time to keep the promise of *equal pay* [*he amplifies his voice*] for an *equal day's work* [*he jabs an index finger in the air; emphasis*], because I want my daughters to have the exact same opportunities as your sons. [*He jabs his index finger again and generates enthusiastic applause.*]

Now, many of these plans will cost money, which is why I've laid out how I'll pay for every dime: by closing corporate loopholes and tax havens that don't help America grow. But I will also go through the federal budget *line by line* [*he punches the words*], eliminating programs that no longer work and making the ones we do need *work better* [*emphasis*] and cost *less* [*emphasis*], because we cannot meet *twenty-first-century* challenges with a *twentieth-century* bureaucracy. [*Applause.*]

And, Democrats—Democrats—we must also admit that fulfilling America's promise will require more than just money. It will require a renewed sense of responsibility [*he softens his tone, speaking the words solemnly and touching his fingertips together*] from each of us to recover what John F. Kennedy called our intellectual and moral strength.

Yes, government must lead on energy independence, but *each of us* [*he stresses each word*] must do our part to make our homes and businesses more efficient. [*Applause.*]

Yes [*emphasis*], we must provide more ladders [*he motions his hands widely*] to success for young men who fall into lives of crime and despair. But we must also admit that programs alone can't replace parents [*his tone is emphatic*], that government can't turn off the television and make a child do her homework [*he motions a hand downward*], that *fathers* must take more responsibility [*he stretches a hand toward the audience, to emphasize the importance*] to provide love and guidance to their children. [*He amplifies his voice and lets the words linger.*]

Individual responsibility [*he pinches the fingers of one hand*] and mutual responsibility [*he pinches the fingers of his other hand, underscoring the significance of the twin responsi-*

bilities], that's the *essence* [*emphasis*] of America's promise. And just as we keep our promise to the next generation here at home, so must we keep America's promise abroad. [*He points an index finger in the air.*]

If John McCain wants to have a debate about who has the *temperament and judgment* [*emphasis*] to serve as the next commander-in-chief, that's a debate I'm ready to have. [*A strong, direct challenge lies beneath his words; his tone is unwavering and he elicits enthusiastic applause.*]

[*He stretches his hand in a stop sign, emphasizing the gravity of the words to follow.*] For while Senator McCain was turning his sights to Iraq [*he stretches his arm and motions his hand, indicating 'far away'*] just days after 9/11, I stood up and opposed this war, knowing that it would distract us from the real threats that we face. [*He points his finger in a chastising manner.*]

When John McCain said we could just muddle through [*he motions his hands, accentuating the words*] in Afghanistan, I argued for more resources and more troops to finish the fight against the terrorists who actually attacked us on 9/11, and made clear that we must *take out* [*he points a finger toward the audience, determinedly*] Osama bin Laden and his lieutenants if we have them in our sights. You know, John McCain likes to say that he'll follow bin Laden to the gates of Hell, but he *won't even follow him to the cave where he lives*. [*He colors his tone with disappointment. Applause.*]

And today, today, as my call for a timeframe to remove our troops from Iraq has been echoed by the Iraqi government and *even* [*emphasis*] the Bush administration, even after we learned that Iraq has $79 *billion* [*emphasis*] in surplus while we are *wallowing* in deficit, John McCain stands alone in his *stubborn* [*emphasis*] refusal to end a misguided war.

That's not the judgment we need [*his tone is indignant*]; that won't keep America safe. We need a president who can face the threats of the future [*his pitch rises*], not keep *grasping* [emphasis] at the ideas of the past. [*He lowers his pitch and stretches an arm, palm downward, conveying disapproval. Applause.*]

You don't defeat a terrorist network that operates in eighty countries by occupying Iraq. [*The audience laughs.*] You don't protect Israel and deter Iran just by talking tough in Washington. [*The audience cheers.*] You can't truly stand up for Georgia when you've strained our oldest alliances.

If John McCain wants to follow George Bush with more tough talk and bad strategy, that is his choice [*he motions both hands to the left—as if indicating their choice is far from him*], but that is not the change that America needs. [*He pinches his fingers. Applause.*]

We are the party of Roosevelt. [*He moves both hands toward his chest and amplifies his voice.*] We are the party of Kennedy. So don't tell me [*he amplifies his voice more, conveying indignation*] that Democrats won't defend this country. *Don't tell me* [*amplified voice*] that Democrats won't keep us safe. [*His tone mocks the notion that Democrats are weak.*]

The Bush-McCain foreign policy has *squandered* [*emphasis*] the legacy that generations of Americans, Democrats *and* [*emphasis*] Republicans, have built, and we are here to restore that legacy. [*He cuts a hand through the air with resoluteness. Applause.*]

As commander-in-chief [*his face is stern*], I will never hesitate to defend this nation, but I will only send our troops into harm's way with a clear mission and a sacred commitment to give them the equipment they need in battle and the care and benefits they deserve when they come home. [*His tone is resolute. Applause.*]

I will end this war in Iraq responsibly and finish the fight against Al Qaida and the Taliban in Afghanistan. I will rebuild [*he points the index finger of one hand toward the audience*] our military to meet future conflicts, but I will also renew the tough, direct diplomacy [*he points the index finger of his other hand toward the audience*] that can prevent Iran from obtaining nuclear weapons and curb Russian aggression.

I will build new partnerships [*he motions his hands widely, signifying the importance*] to defeat the threats of the twenty-first century: terrorism and nuclear proliferation, poverty and genocide, climate change and disease.

And I will *restore* [*emphasis*] our moral standing so that America [*he slices his hand through the air*] is once again that *last, best hope* [*emphasis*] for *all* [*he stretches his arm, palm down, emphasizing the word*] who are called to the cause of freedom, who *long* [*emphasis*] for lives of peace, and who *yearn* [*emphasis*] for a better future. [*He progressively amplifies his voice for great effect and he generates tremendous applause. The audience begins chanting "USA! USA!"*]

These [*emphasis*] are the policies I will pursue. And in the weeks ahead, I look forward to debating them with John McCain. [*His tone is determined.*]

But [*pause*] what I will *not* do is suggest that the senator takes his positions for political purposes [*his tone rings with moral rightness*], because one of the things that we have to change in our politics is the idea that people cannot disagree without challenging each other's character and each other's patriotism. [*Applause.*]

The times are too serious [*pause*], the stakes are too high for this same partisan playbook. So let us agree that patriotism has no party. I love this country [*he places a hand to his chest*], and so do you [*he points his finger toward the audience*], and so does John McCain. [*He point his finger again, indicating McCain.*]

The men and women who serve in our battlefields may be Democrats *and* Republicans *and* Independents, but they have fought together, *and bled* together, *and* some *died* together under the same *proud* flag. They have not served a *red* [*emphasis*] America or a *blue* [*emphasis*] America; they have served the *United States of America* [*he thumps a finger against the lectern emphatically and enunciates each word: U-ni-ted-States-of-A-mer-i-ca. The audience erupts in thunderous applause and chants "USA! USA!" Listeners wave flags throughout the stadium.*]

[*He motions a vertical palm in a stop sign.*] So I've got news for you, John McCain [*his face is stern; he amplifies his voice, making his challenge is clear*]: We *all* [*emphasis*] put our country first. [*He cuts a hand through the air. Dramatic pause. Applause.*]

America, our work will not be easy. The challenges we face require tough choices. And Democrats, as well as Republicans, will need to cast off the worn-out ideas [*he motions a hand as if pushing away the antiquated ideas*] and politics of the past, for part of what has been lost these past eight years can't just be measured by lost wages or bigger trade deficits. What has also been lost is our sense of common purpose [*he softens his voice, giving the words gravity*], and *that's* [*emphasis*] what we have to restore.

We may not agree on abortion, but surely we can agree on reducing the number of unwanted pregnancies in this country. [*He quickens his cadence to underscore the point. Applause.*]

The reality of gun ownership may be different for hunters in rural Ohio than they are for those plagued by gang violence in Cleveland, *but* [*emphasis*] don't tell me we can't uphold the Second Amendment while keeping AK-47s out of the hands of criminals. [*His tone ridicules any notion this cannot be done and generates applause.*]

I know there are differences on same-sex marriage, but *surely* [*emphasis*] we can agree that our gay and lesbian brothers and sisters deserve to visit the person they love in a hospital and to live lives free of discrimination. [*Applause.*]

You know, passions may fly on immigration, but I don't know anyone who benefits when a mother is separated from her infant child [*he motions his hands apart*] or an employer undercuts American wages by hiring illegal workers.

But this, too, is part of America's promise [*he touches his hands together gently, underscoring the preciousness of the promise*], the promise of a democracy where we can find the strength [*slight pause*] and grace [*his voice lingers on the "c," highlighting the word 'grace'*] to bridge divides and unite in common effort.

I know there are those who dismiss such beliefs as happy talk. They claim that our insistence on something *larger* [*slight pause*], something *firmer*, and more *honest* in our public life is just a Trojan horse for higher taxes and the abandonment of traditional values. And that's to be expected, because if you don't have any fresh ideas, then you use stale tactics to scare voters. [*He points a finger accusingly. Applause.*]

If you don't have a record to run on [*he wags an index finger back and forth*], then you paint your opponent as someone people should run *from* [*emphasis*]. You make a big election [*he moves both hands apart, indicating something large*] about small things [*he brings his hands together, motioning to indicate smallness*]. And you know what? It's worked before, because it *feeds* into the cynicism we all have about government. When Washington doesn't work, all its promises seem empty [*he motions a hand away, as if pushing a false promise far away*]. If your hopes have been dashed again and again, then it's best to stop hoping and settle for what you already know. [*His pitch dips slightly, conveying disapproval.*]

I get it. I realize that I am not the likeliest candidate for this office [*he moves both hands toward his chest*]. I don't fit the typical pedigree, and I haven't spent my career in the halls of Washington. But I stand before you tonight because all across America something is stirring [*he motions his hands widely*]. What the naysayers don't understand is that this election has never been about me [*his pitch dips and he pauses*]; it's about you. [*His pitch rises; he points a finger toward the audience. Enthusiastic applause.*]

It's about you. [*More applause.*]

For eighteen long months, you have stood up, *one by one*, and said, "*Enough*," [*emphasis*] to the politics of the past. *You* [*he draws out the word and points a finger at the audience*] understand that, in this election, the greatest risk we can take is to try the *same, old politics* with the *same, old players* [*emphasis*] and expect a different result.

You have shown what history teaches us—that at defining moments like this one, the change we need doesn't come *from* [*emphasis*] Washington. Change comes *to* [*emphasis*] Washington. [*He motions his hands widely. Applause.*]

Change [*he nearly sings the word and cuts a hand through the air, adding emphasis*] happens—change happens because the American people *demand* it, because they *rise up* [*he motions his hands emphatically*] and insist on *new* ideas [*slight pause*] and *new* leadership [*slight pause*], a *new* politics [*he slices a hand through the air*] for a *new* time. [*He pinches his fingers.*]

America, this is one of those moments.

I believe [*he nearly sings the words, letting them linger*] that, as hard as it will be [*slight pause*], the change we need is coming [*he dips his pitch*], because I've *seen* it [*he motions his hands to his chest; slight pause for impact*], because I've *lived* it. [*Slight pause.*]

Because I've seen it in Illinois, when we provided health care to more children [*he motions his hands widely*] and moved more families from welfare to work. I've seen it in Washington, where we worked across party lines to open up government and hold lobbyists more accountable, to give better care for our veterans, and keep nuclear weapons out of the hands of terrorists. [*He glides his voice up and down to emphasize the breadth of change.*] And I've *seen* it in this campaign [*his tone is filled with admiration*], in the young people who voted for the *first time* [*pride sounds in his voice*] and the young at heart, those who got involved again after a *very long* time; in the Republicans who never thought [*slight chuckle, slight smile*] they'd pick up a Democratic ballot [*he gives a dramatic pause to underscore the importance*], but did. [*He smiles. Applause.*]

I've seen it—I've seen it in the workers who would rather cut their hours back a day [*he pinches his fingers*], even though they can't afford it, than see their friends lose their jobs; in the soldiers who re-enlist after losing a limb; in the good neighbors who take a stranger in when a hurricane strikes and the floodwaters rise.

You know, this country of ours has more wealth than any nation, but that's not what makes us rich. We have the most powerful military on Earth, but that's not what makes us strong [*his pitch rises and falls, underscoring his point*]. Our universities and our culture are the envy of the world [*his pitch crests; he motions his hands wide, signifying the grandness of the USA*], but that's not what keeps the world coming to our shores [*his pitch dips*].

Instead [*he dips his voice again*], it is that American spirit [*pause*], that American promise, that pushes us forward even when the path is uncertain; that binds us together in spite of our differences; that makes us fix our eye not on what is seen, but what is *unseen* [*emphasis*], that better place around the bend. [*His tone is wistful and filled with hope.*]

That promise [*his voice lingers on the "s," emphasizing 'promise'*] is our greatest inheritance. It's a promise I make to my daughters when I tuck them in at night and a promise [*his voice stresses the "s," highlighting the word 'promise'*] that you make to yours, a promise that has led immigrants to *cross oceans* [*he amplifies his voice, highlighting the greatness of this*] and pioneers to travel west, a promise that led workers to picket lines and women to reach for the ballot. [*He quickens his cadence; his pitch rises and falls. Applause.*]

And [*slight pause*] it is that promise that, forty-five years ago today [*pause*], brought Americans from every corner of this land to *stand together* on a Mall in Washington, before Lincoln's Memorial, and hear a young preacher from Georgia speak of his dream [*he progressively amplifies his voice, giving great effect to his words and rousing listeners with his reference to Martin Luther King Jr. He lets the words linger. The audience rings with enthusiastic applause.*]

The men and women who gathered there could've heard many things. They could've heard words of anger and discord. They could've been told to succumb to the *fear and frustrations* of so many dreams deferred.

But what the people heard instead—people of every *creed and color*, from every walk of life—is that, *in America* [*emphasis*], our destiny is inextricably linked, *that together* [*emphasis*] our dreams can be one. [*He pinches his fingers, accentuating the points.*]

"*We cannot walk alone,*" [*he slices his hand emphatically through the air*] the preacher cried. "And as we walk, we must make the pledge that we shall always march ahead. [*He cuts his hand through the air again.*] *We cannot turn back.*" [*He stresses each word.*]

America, we cannot turn back . . . [*His tone remains determined; he wags his index finger high in the air. Applause.*] . . . *Not* [*emphasis*] with so much work to be done [*he amplifies his volume and keeps it raised and he points repeatedly to the audience, challenging listeners*]; *not* [*emphasis*] with so many children to educate, and so many veterans to care for; *not* [*emphasis*] with an economy to fix, *and* cities to rebuild, *and* farms to save; *not* [*emphasis*] with so many families to protect and so many lives to mend.

America! We cannot turn back. [*His tone issues a challenge. Pause.*] We cannot walk alone. [*His tone is unwavering and resolute as he builds to a crescendo.*]

At this moment, in this election [*his tone underscores a sense of urgency as he reaches his crescendo*], we must pledge once more to march into the future. Let us *keep* [*emphasis*] that promise [*his tone issues a challenge*], that *American promise* [*his tone is wistful*], and in the words of Scripture hold firmly [*he speaks the word "Scripture" with reverence*], without *wavering*, to the hope that we confess.

Thank you! [*Slight pause.*] God bless you! [*Slight pause.*] And *God bless* [*emphasis*] the United States of America! [*Emphases added.*]

[*The audience rises in an ovation. Obama stretches his arm wide, waving to the audience. He claps his hands briefly with the audience, underscoring their unity. The audience continues on in applause.*]

The media, many listeners and political pundits immediately praised Barack Obama's 2008 presidential nomination acceptance speech as "magnificent," "extraordinary," "electrifying," "rousing," "unifying," and "the best since President Kennedy." The masterful and powerful delivery solidified Obama's place as one of the most effective and outstanding orators of recent times.

Were you able to identify all of the rhetorical techniques? For more extensive analysis of this historic speech and discussion about the valuable rhetorical techniques in this masterful acceptance address, visit www.shelleanne.com or www.sayitlikeobama.com.

⇥ ELECTION NIGHT VICTORY SPEECH ⇤
GRANT PARK, CHICAGO
NOVEMBER 4, 2008

If there is anyone out there who still doubts that America is a place where all things are possible; who still wonders if the dream of our founders is alive in our time; who still questions the power of our democracy, tonight is your answer.

It's the answer told by lines that stretched around schools and churches in numbers this nation has never seen; by people who waited three hours and four hours, many for the very first time in their lives, because they believed that this time must be different; that their voice could be that difference.

It's the answer spoken by young and old, rich and poor, Democrat and Republican, black, white, Latino, Asian, Native American, gay, straight, disabled and not disabled—Americans who sent a message to the world that we have never been a collection of Red States and Blue States: we are, and always will be, the United States of America.

It's the answer that led those who have been told for so long by so many to be cynical, and fearful, and doubtful of what we can achieve to put their hands on the arc of history and bend it once more toward the hope of a better day.

It's been a long time coming, but tonight, because of what we did on this day, in this election, at this defining moment, change has come to America.

I just received a very gracious call from Senator McCain. He fought long and hard in this campaign, and he's fought even longer and harder for the country he loves. He has endured sacrifices for America that most of us cannot begin to imagine, and we are better off for the service rendered by this brave and selfless leader. I congratulate him and Governor Palin for all they have achieved, and I look forward to working with them to renew this nation's promise in the months ahead.

I want to thank my partner in this journey, a man who campaigned from his heart and spoke for the men and women he grew up with on the streets of Scranton and rode with on that train home to Delaware, the Vice President-elect of the United States, Joe Biden.

I would not be standing here tonight without the unyielding support of my best friend for the last sixteen years, the rock of our family and the love of my life, our nation's next First Lady, Michelle Obama. Sasha and Malia, I love you both so much, and you have earned the new puppy that's coming with us to the White House. And while she's no longer with us, I know my grandmother is watching, along with the family that made me who I am. I miss them tonight, and know that my debt to them is beyond measure.

To my campaign manager David Plouffe, my chief strategist David Axelrod, and the best campaign team ever assembled in the history of politics—you made this happen, and I am forever grateful for what you've sacrificed to get it done.

But above all, I will never forget who this victory truly belongs to—it belongs to you.

I was never the likeliest candidate for this office. We didn't start with much money or many endorsements. Our campaign was not hatched in the halls of Washington—it began in the backyards of Des Moines and the living rooms of Concord and the front porches of Charleston.

It was built by working men and women who dug into what little savings they had to give five dollars and ten dollars and twenty dollars to this cause. It grew strength from the young people who rejected the myth of their generation's apathy; who left their homes and their families for jobs that offered little pay and less sleep; from the not-so-young people who braved the bitter cold and scorching heat to knock on the doors of perfect strangers; from the millions of Americans who volunteered, and organized, and proved that more than two centuries later, a government of the people, by the people and for the people has not perished from this Earth. This is your victory. I know you didn't do this just to win an election and I know you didn't do it for me. You did it because you understand the enormity of the task that lies ahead. For even as we celebrate tonight, we know the challenges that tomorrow will bring are the greatest of our lifetime—two wars, a planet in peril, the worst financial crisis in a century. Even as we stand here tonight, we know there are brave Americans waking up in the deserts of Iraq and the mountains of Afghanistan to risk their lives for us. There are mothers and fathers who will lie awake after their children fall asleep and wonder how they'll make the mortgage, or pay their doctor's bills, or save enough for college. There is new energy to harness and new jobs to be created; new schools to build and threats to meet and alliances to repair.

The road ahead will be long. Our climb will be steep. We may not get there in one year or even one term, but America—I have never been more hopeful than I am tonight that we will get there. I promise you—we as a people will get there.

There will be setbacks and false starts. There are many who won't agree with every decision or policy I make as President, and we know that government can't solve every problem. But I will always be honest with you about the challenges we face. I will listen to you, especially when we disagree. And above all, I will ask you join in the work of remaking this nation the only way it's been done in America for two-hundred and twenty-one years—block by block, brick by brick, calloused hand by calloused hand.

What began twenty-one months ago in the depths of winter must not end on this autumn night. This victory alone is not the change we seek—it is only the chance for us to make that change. And that cannot happen if we go back to the way things were. It cannot happen without you.

So let us summon a new spirit of patriotism; of service and responsibility where each of us resolves to pitch in and work harder and look after not only ourselves, but each other. Let us remember that if this financial crisis taught us anything, it's that we cannot have a thriving Wall Street while Main Street suffers—in this country, we rise or fall as one nation; as one people.

Let us resist the temptation to fall back on the same partisanship and pettiness and immaturity that has poisoned our politics for so long. Let us remember that it was a man from this state who first carried the banner of the Republican Party to the White House—a party founded on the values of self-reliance, individual liberty, and national unity. Those are values we all share, and while the Democratic Party has won a great victory tonight, we do so with a measure of humility and determination to heal the divides that have held back our progress. As Lincoln said to a nation far more divided than ours, "We are not enemies, but friends...though passion may have strained it must not break our bonds of affection." And to those Americans whose support I have yet to earn—I may not have won your vote, but I hear your voices, I need your help, and I will be your President too.

And to all those watching tonight from beyond our shores, from parliaments and palaces to those who are huddled around radios in the forgotten corners of our world— our stories are singular, but our destiny is shared, and a new dawn of American leadership is at hand. To those who would tear this world down—we will defeat you. To those who seek peace and security—we support you. And to all those who have wondered if America's beacon still burns bright—tonight we proved once more that the true strength of our nation comes not from our the might of our arms or the scale of our wealth, but from the enduring power of our ideals: democracy, liberty, opportunity, and unyielding hope.

For that is the true genius of America—that America can change. Our union can be perfected. And what we have already achieved gives us hope for what we can and must achieve tomorrow.

This election had many firsts and many stories that will be told for generations. But one that's on my mind tonight is about a woman who cast her ballot in Atlanta. She's a lot like the millions of others who stood in line to make their voice heard in this election except for one thing—Ann Nixon Cooper is 106 years old.

She was born just a generation past slavery; a time when there were no cars on the road or planes in the sky; when someone like her couldn't vote for two reasons—because she was a woman and because of the color of her skin.

And tonight, I think about all that she's seen throughout her century in America—the heartache and the hope; the struggle and the progress; the times we were told that we can't, and the people who pressed on with that American creed: Yes we can.

At a time when women's voices were silenced and their hopes dismissed, she lived to see them stand up and speak out and reach for the ballot. Yes we can.

When there was despair in the dust bowl and depression across the land, she saw a nation conquer fear itself with a New Deal, new jobs, and a new sense of common purpose. Yes we can.

When the bombs fell on our harbor and tyranny threatened the world, she was there to witness a generation rise to greatness and a democracy was saved. Yes we can.

She was there for the buses in Montgomery, the hoses in Birmingham, a bridge in Selma, and a preacher from Atlanta who told a people that "We Shall Overcome." Yes we can.

A man touched down on the moon, a wall came down in Berlin, a world was connected by our own science and imagination. And this year, in this election, she touched her finger to a screen, and cast her vote, because after 106 years in America, through the best of times and the darkest of hours, she knows how America can change. Yes we can.

America, we have come so far. We have seen so much. But there is so much more to do. So tonight, let us ask ourselves—if our children should live to see the next century; if my daughters should be so lucky to live as long as Ann Nixon Cooper, what change will they see? What progress will we have made?

This is our chance to answer that call. This is our moment. This is our time—to put our people back to work and open doors of opportunity for our kids; to restore prosperity and promote the cause of peace; to reclaim the American Dream and reaffirm that fundamental truth—that out of many, we are one; that while we breathe, we hope, and where we are met with cynicism, and doubt, and those who tell us that we can't, we will respond with that timeless creed that sums up the spirit of a people:

Yes We Can. Thank you, God bless you, and may God bless the United States of America.

⇥ Barack Obama's Inaugural Address ⇤

My fellow citizens: I stand here today humbled by the task before us, grateful for the trust you've bestowed, mindful of the sacrifices borne by our ancestors.

I thank President Bush for his service to our nation—(applause)—as well as the generosity and cooperation he has shown throughout this transition.

Forty-four Americans have now taken the presidential oath. The words have been spoken during rising tides of prosperity and the still waters of peace. Yet, every so often, the oath is taken amidst gathering clouds and raging storms. At these moments, America has carried on not simply because of the skill or vision of those in high office, but because we, the people, have remained faithful to the ideals of our forebears and true to our founding documents.

So it has been; so it must be with this generation of Americans.

That we are in the midst of crisis is now well understood. Our nation is at war against a far-reaching network of violence and hatred. Our economy is badly weakened, a consequence of greed and irresponsibility on the part of some, but also our collective failure to make hard choices and prepare the nation for a new age. Homes have been lost, jobs shed, businesses shuttered. Our health care is too costly, our schools fail too many—and each day brings further evidence that the ways we use energy strengthen our adversaries and threaten our planet.

These are the indicators of crisis, subject to data and statistics. Less measurable, but no less profound, is a sapping of confidence across our land; a nagging fear that America's decline is inevitable, that the next generation must lower its sights.

Today I say to you that the challenges we face are real. They are serious and they are many. They will not be met easily or in a short span of time. But know this America: They will be met. [*Applause.*]

On this day, we gather because we have chosen hope over fear, unity of purpose over conflict and discord. On this day, we come to proclaim an end to the petty grievances and false promises, the recriminations and worn-out dogmas that for far too long have strangled our politics. We remain a young nation. But in the words of Scripture, the time has come to set aside childish things. The time has come to reaffirm our enduring spirit; to choose our better history; to carry forward that precious gift, that noble idea passed on from generation to generation: the God-given promise that all are equal, all are free, and all deserve a chance to pursue their full measure of happiness. [*Applause.*]

In reaffirming the greatness of our nation we understand that greatness is never a given. It must be earned. Our journey has never been one of short-cuts or settling for less. It has not been the path for the faint-hearted, for those that prefer leisure over work, or seek only the pleasures of riches and fame. Rather, it has been the risk-takers, the doers, the makers of things—some celebrated, but more often men and women obscure in their labor—who have carried us up the long rugged path towards prosperity and freedom.

For us, they packed up their few worldly possessions and traveled across oceans in search of a new life. For us, they toiled in sweatshops, and settled the West, endured the lash of the whip, and plowed the hard earth. For us, they fought and died in places like Concord and Gettysburg, Normandy and Khe Sahn.

Time and again these men and women struggled and sacrificed and worked till their hands were raw so that we might live a better life. They saw America as bigger than the sum of our individual ambitions, greater than all the differences of birth or wealth or faction.

This is the journey we continue today. We remain the most prosperous, powerful nation on Earth. Our workers are no less productive than when this crisis began. Our minds are no less inventive, our goods and services no less needed than they were last week, or last month, or last year. Our capacity remains undiminished. But our time of standing pat, of protecting narrow interests and putting off unpleasant decisions—that time has surely passed. Starting today, we must pick ourselves up, dust ourselves off, and begin again the work of remaking America. [*Applause.*]

For everywhere we look, there is work to be done. The state of our economy calls for action, bold and swift. And we will act, not only to create new jobs, but to lay a new foundation for growth. We will build the roads and bridges, the electric grids and digital lines that feed our commerce and bind us together. We'll restore science to its rightful place, and wield technology's wonders to raise health care's quality and lower its cost. We will harness the sun and the winds and the soil to fuel our cars and run our factories. And we will transform our schools and colleges and universities to meet the demands of a new age. All this we can do. All this we will do.

Now, there are some who question the scale of our ambitions, who suggest that our system cannot tolerate too many big plans. Their memories are short, for they have forgotten what this country has already done, what free men and women can achieve when imagination is joined to common purpose, and necessity to courage. What the cynics fail to understand is that the ground has shifted beneath them, that the stale political arguments that have consumed us for so long no longer apply.

The question we ask today is not whether our government is too big or too small, but whether it works—whether it helps families find jobs at a decent wage, care they can afford, a retirement that is dignified. Where the answer is yes, we intend to move forward. Where the answer is no, programs will end. And those of us who manage the public's dollars will be held to account, to spend wisely, reform bad habits, and do our business in the light of day, because only then can we restore the vital trust between a people and their government.

Nor is the question before us whether the market is a force for good or ill. Its power to generate wealth and expand freedom is unmatched. But this crisis has reminded us that without a watchful eye, the market can spin out of control. The nation cannot prosper long when it favors only the prosperous. The success of our economy has always depended not just on the size of our gross domestic product, but on the reach of our prosperity, on the ability to extend opportunity to every willing heart—not out of charity, but because it is the surest route to our common good. [*Applause.*]

As for our common defense, we reject as false the choice between our safety and our ideals. Our Founding Fathers—[*applause*]—our Founding Fathers, faced with perils that we can scarcely imagine, drafted a charter to assure the rule of law and the rights of man—a charter expanded by the blood of generations. Those ideals still light the world, and we will not give them up for expedience sake. [*Applause.*]

And so, to all the other peoples and governments who are watching today, from the grandest capitals to the small village where my father was born, know that America is a friend of each nation, and every man, woman and child who seeks a future of peace and dignity. And we are ready to lead once more. [*Applause.*]

Recall that earlier generations faced down fascism and communism not just with missiles and tanks, but with the sturdy alliances and enduring convictions. They understood that our power alone cannot protect us, nor does it entitle us to do as we please. Instead they knew that our power grows through its prudent use; our security emanates from the justness of our cause, the force of our example, the tempering qualities of humility and restraint.

We are the keepers of this legacy. Guided by these principles once more we can meet those new threats that demand even greater effort, even greater cooperation and understanding between nations. We will begin to responsibly leave Iraq to its people and forge a hard-earned peace in Afghanistan. With old friends and former foes, we'll work tirelessly to lessen the nuclear threat, and roll back the specter of a warming planet.

We will not apologize for our way of life, nor will we waver in its defense. And for those who seek to advance their aims by inducing terror and slaughtering innocents, we say to you now that our spirit is stronger and cannot be broken—you cannot outlast us, and we will defeat you. [*Applause.*]

For we know that our patchwork heritage is a strength, not a weakness. We are a nation of Christians and Muslims, Jews and Hindus, and non-believers. We are shaped by every language and culture, drawn from every end of this Earth; and because we have tasted the bitter swill of civil war and segregation, and emerged from that dark chapter stronger and more united, we cannot help but believe that the old hatreds shall someday pass; that the lines of tribe shall soon dissolve; that as the world grows smaller, our common humanity shall reveal itself; and that America must play its role in ushering in a new era of peace.

To the Muslim world, we seek a new way forward, based on mutual interest and mutual respect. To those leaders around the globe who seek to sow conflict, or blame their society's ills on the West, know that your people will judge you on what you can build, not what you destroy. [*Applause.*]

To those who cling to power through corruption and deceit and the silencing of dissent, know that you are on the wrong side of history, but that we will extend a hand if you are willing to unclench your fist. [*Applause.*]

To the people of poor nations, we pledge to work alongside you to make your farms flourish and let clean waters flow; to nourish starved bodies and feed hungry minds. And to those nations like ours that enjoy relative plenty, we say we can no longer afford indifference to the suffering outside our borders, nor can we consume the world's resources without regard to effect. For the world has changed, and we must change with it.

As we consider the role that unfolds before us, we remember with humble gratitude those brave Americans who at this very hour patrol far-off deserts and distant mountains. They have something to tell us, just as the fallen heroes who lie in Arlington whisper through the ages.

We honor them not only because they are the guardians of our liberty, but because they embody the spirit of service—a willingness to find meaning in something greater than themselves.

And yet at this moment, a moment that will define a generation, it is precisely this spirit that must inhabit us all. For as much as government can do, and must do, it is ultimately the faith and determination of the American people upon which this nation relies. It is the kindness to take in a stranger when the levees break, the selflessness of workers who would rather cut their hours than see a friend lose their job which sees us through our darkest hours. It is the firefighter's courage to storm a stairway filled with smoke, but also a parent's willingness to nurture a child that finally decides our fate.

Our challenges may be new. The instruments with which we meet them may be new. But those values upon which our success depends—honesty and hard work, courage and fair play, tolerance and curiosity, loyalty and patriotism—these things are old. These things are true. They have been the quiet force of progress throughout our history.

What is demanded, then, is a return to these truths. What is required of us now is a new era of responsibility— a recognition on the part of every American that we have duties to ourselves, our nation and the world; duties that we do not grudgingly accept, but rather seize gladly, firm in the knowledge that there is nothing so satisfying to the spirit, so defining of our character than giving our all to a difficult task.

This is the price and the promise of citizenship. This is the source of our confidence—the knowledge that God calls on us to shape an uncertain destiny. This is the meaning of our liberty and our creed, why men and women and children of every race and every faith can join in celebration across this magnificent mall; and why a man whose father less than 60 years ago might not have been served in a local restaurant can now stand before you to take a most sacred oath. [*Applause.*]

So let us mark this day with remembrance of who we are and how far we have traveled. In the year of America's birth, in the coldest of months, a small band of patriots huddled by dying campfires on the shores of an icy river. The capital was abandoned. The enemy was advancing. The snow was stained with blood. At the moment when the outcome of our revolution was most in doubt, the father of our nation ordered these words to be read to the people:

"Let it be told to the future world . . . that in the depth of winter, when nothing but hope and virtue could survive . . . that the city and the country, alarmed at one common danger, came forth to meet [it]."

America: In the face of our common dangers, in this winter of our hardship, let us remember these timeless words. With hope and virtue, let us brave once more the icy currents, and endure what storms may come. Let it be said by our children's children that when we were tested we refused to let this journey end, that we did not turn back nor did we falter; and with eyes fixed on the horizon and God's grace upon us, we carried forth that great gift of freedom and delivered it safely to future generations.

Thank you. God bless you. And God bless the United States of America. [*Applause.*]

⇥ ADDRESS TO GHANA'S PARLIAMENT ⇤
JULY 11, 2009

Good morning. It is an honor for me to be in Accra, and to speak to the representatives of the people of Ghana. I am deeply grateful for the welcome that I've received, as are Michelle, Malia, and Sasha Obama. Ghana's history is rich, the ties between our two countries are strong, and I am proud that this is my first visit to sub-Saharan Africa as President of the United States.

I am speaking to you at the end of a long trip. I began in Russia, for a Summit between two great powers. I traveled to Italy, for a meeting of the world's leading economies. And I have come here, to Ghana, for a simple reason: the twenty-first century will be shaped by what happens not just in Rome or Moscow or Washington, but by what happens in Accra as well.

This is the simple truth of a time when the boundaries between people are overwhelmed by our connections. Your prosperity can expand America's. Your health and security can contribute to the world's. And the strength of your democracy can help advance human rights for people everywhere.

So I do not see the countries and peoples of Africa as a world apart; I see Africa as a fundamental part of our inter-connected world—as partners with America on behalf of the future that we want for all our children. That partnership must be grounded in mutual responsibility, and that is what I want to speak with you about today.

We must start from the simple premise that Africa's future is up to Africans.

I say this knowing full well the tragic past that has sometimes haunted this part of the world. I have the blood of Africa within me, and my family's own story encompasses both the tragedies and triumphs of the larger African story.

My grandfather was a cook for the British in Kenya, and though he was a respected elder in his village, his employers called him "boy" for much of his life. He was on the periphery of Kenya's liberation struggles, but he was still imprisoned briefly during repressive times. In his life, colonialism wasn't simply the creation of unnatural borders or unfair terms of trade—it was something experienced personally, day after day, year after year.

My father grew up herding goats in a tiny village, an impossible distance away from the American universities where he would come to get an education. He came of age at an extraordinary moment of promise for Africa. The struggles of his own father's generation were giving birth to new nations, beginning right here in Ghana. Africans were educating and asserting themselves in new ways. History was on the move. But despite the progress that has been made—and there has been considerable progress in parts of Africa—we also know that much of that promise has yet to be fulfilled. Countries like Kenya, which had a per capita economy larger than South Korea's when I was born, have been badly outpaced. Disease and conflict have ravaged parts of the African continent. In many places, the hope of my father's generation gave way to cynicism, even despair.

It is easy to point fingers, and to pin the blame for these problems on others. Yes, a colonial map that made little sense bred conflict, and the West has often approached Africa as a patron, rather than a partner. But the West is not responsible for the destruction of the Zimbabwean economy over the last decade, or wars in which children are enlisted as combatants. In my father's life, it was partly tribalism and patronage in an independent Kenya that for a long stretch derailed his career, and we know that this kind of corruption is a daily fact of life for far too many.

Of course, we also know that is not the whole story. Here in Ghana, you show us a face of Africa that is too often overlooked by a world that sees only tragedy or the need for charity. The people of Ghana have worked hard to put democracy on a firmer footing, with peaceful transfers of power even in the wake of closely contested elections. And with improved governance and an emerging civil society, Ghana's economy has shown impressive rates of growth.

This progress may lack the drama of the twentieth century's liberation struggles, but make no mistake: it will ultimately be more significant. For just as it is important to emerge from the control of another nation, it is even more important to build one's own.

So I believe that this moment is just as promising for Ghana—and for Africa—as the moment when my father came of age and new nations were being born. This is a new moment of promise. Only this time, we have learned that it will not be giants like Nkrumah and Kenyatta who will determine Africa's future. Instead, it will be you—the men and women in Ghana's Parliament, and the people you represent. Above all, it will be the young people—brimming with talent and energy and hope—who can claim the future that so many in my father's generation never found.

To realize that promise, we must first recognize a fundamental truth that you have given life to in Ghana: development depends upon good governance. That is the ingredient which has been missing in far too many places, for far too long. That is the change that can unlock Africa's potential. And that is a responsibility that can only be met by Africans.

As for America and the West, our commitment must be measured by more than just the dollars we spend. I have pledged substantial increases in our foreign assistance, which is in Africa's interest and America's. But the true sign of success is not whether we are a source of aid that helps people scrape by—it is whether we are partners in building the capacity for transformational change.

This mutual responsibility must be the foundation of our partnership. And today, I will focus on four areas that are critical to the future of Africa and the entire developing world: democracy; opportunity; health; and the peaceful resolution of conflict.

First, we must support strong and sustainable democratic governments.

As I said in Cairo, each nation gives life to democracy in its own way, and in line with its own traditions. But history offers a clear verdict: governments that respect the will of their own people are more prosperous, more stable, and more successful than governments that do not.

This is about more than holding elections—it's also about what happens between them. Repression takes many forms, and too many nations are plagued by problems that condemn their people to poverty. No country is going to create wealth if its leaders exploit the economy to enrich themselves, or police can be bought off by drug traffickers. No business wants to invest in a place where the government skims 20 percent off the top, or the head of the Port Authority is corrupt. No person wants to live in a society where the rule of law gives way to the rule of brutality and bribery. That is not democracy, that is tyranny, and now is the time for it to end.

In the twenty-first century, capable, reliable and transparent institutions are the key to success—strong parliaments and honest police forces; independent judges and journalists; a vibrant private sector and civil society. Those are the things that give life to democracy, because that is what matters in peoples' lives.

Time and again, Ghanaians have chosen Constitutional rule over autocracy, and shown a democratic spirit that allows the energy of your people to break through. We see that in leaders who accept defeat graciously, and victors who resist calls to wield power against the opposition. We see that spirit in courageous journalists like Anas Aremeyaw Anas, who risked his life to report the truth. We see it in police like Patience Quaye, who helped prosecute the first human trafficker in Ghana. We see it in the young people who are speaking up against patronage, and participating in the political process.

Across Africa, we have seen countless examples of people taking control of their destiny, and making change from the bottom up. We saw it in Kenya, where civil society and business came together to help stop post-election violence. We saw it in South Africa, where over three quarters of the country voted in the recent election— the fourth since the end of Apartheid. We saw it in Zimbabwe, where the Election Support Network braved brutal repression to stand up for the principle that a person's vote is their sacred right.

Make no mistake: history is on the side of these brave Africans, and not with those who use coups or change Constitutions to stay in power. Africa doesn't need strongmen, it needs strong institutions.

America will not seek to impose any system of government on any other nation—the essential truth of democracy is that each nation determines its own destiny. What we will do is increase assistance for responsible individuals and institutions, with a focus on supporting good governance— on parliaments, which check abuses of power and ensure that opposition voices are heard; on the rule of law, which ensures the equal administration of justice; on civic participation, so that young people get involved; and on concrete solutions to corruption like forensic accounting, automating services, strengthening hotlines, and protecting whistleblowers to advance transparency and accountability.

As we provide this support, I have directed my Administration to give greater attention to corruption in our Human Rights report. People everywhere should have the right to start a business or get an education without paying a bribe. We have a responsibility to support those who act responsibly and to isolate those who don't, and that is exactly what America will do.

This leads directly to our second area of partnership— supporting development that provides opportunity for more people.

With better governance, I have no doubt that Africa holds the promise of a broader base for prosperity. The continent is rich in natural resources. And from cell phone entrepreneurs to small farmers, Africans have shown the capacity and commitment to create their own opportunities. But old habits must also be broken. Dependence on commodities—or on a single export—concentrates wealth in the hands of the few, and leaves people too vulnerable to downturns.

In Ghana, for instance, oil brings great opportunities, and you have been responsible in preparing for new revenue. But as so many Ghanaians know, oil cannot simply become the new cocoa. From South Korea to Singapore, history shows that countries thrive when they invest in their people and infrastructure; when they promote multiple export industries, develop a skilled workforce, and create space for small and medium-sized businesses that create jobs.

As Africans reach for this promise, America will be more responsible in extending our hand. By cutting costs that go to Western consultants and administration, we will put more resources in the hands of those who need it, while training people to do more for themselves. That is why our $3.5 billion food security initiative is focused on new methods and technologies for farmers—not simply sending American producers or goods to Africa. Aid is not an end in itself. The purpose of foreign assistance must be creating the conditions where it is no longer needed.

America can also do more to promote trade and investment. Wealthy nations must open our doors to goods and services from Africa in a meaningful way. And where there is good governance, we can broaden prosperity through public-private partnerships that invest in better roads and electricity; capacity-building that trains people to grow a business; and financial services that reach poor and rural areas. This is also in our own interest—for if people are lifted out of poverty and wealth is created in Africa, new markets will open for our own goods.

One area that holds out both undeniable peril and extraordinary promise is energy. Africa gives off less greenhouse gas than any other part of the world, but it is the most threatened by climate change. A warming planet will spread disease, shrink water resources, and deplete crops, creating conditions that produce more famine and conflict. All of us—particularly the developed world—have a responsibility to slow these trends—through mitigation, and by changing the way that we use energy. But we can also work with Africans to turn this crisis into opportunity.

Together, we can partner on behalf of our planet and prosperity, and help countries increase access to power while skipping the dirtier phase of development. Across Africa, there is bountiful wind and solar power; geothermal energy and bio-fuels. From the Rift Valley to the North African deserts; from the Western coast to South Africa's crops— Africa's boundless natural gifts can generate its own power, while exporting profitable, clean energy abroad.

These steps are about more than growth numbers on a balance sheet. They're about whether a young person with an education can get a job that supports a family; a farmer can transfer their goods to the market; or an entrepreneur with a good idea can start a business. It's about the dignity of work. It's about the opportunity that must exist for Africans in the twenty-first century.

Just as governance is vital to opportunity, it is also critical to the third area that I will talk about—strengthening public health.

In recent years, enormous progress has been made in parts of Africa. Far more people are living productively with HIV/AIDS, and getting the drugs they need. But too many still die from diseases that shouldn't kill them. When children are being killed because of a mosquito bite, and mothers are dying in childbirth, then we know that more progress must be made.

Yet because of incentives—often provided by donor nations—many African doctors and nurses understandably go overseas, or work for programs that focus on a single disease. This creates gaps in primary care and basic prevention. Meanwhile, individual Africans also have to make responsible choices that prevent the spread of disease, while promoting public health in their communities and countries.

Across Africa, we see examples of people tackling these problems. In Nigeria, an Interfaith effort of Christians and Muslims has set an example of cooperation to confront malaria. Here in Ghana and across Africa, we see innovative ideas for filling gaps in care—for instance, through E-Health initiatives that allow doctors in big cities to support those in small towns.

America will support these efforts through a comprehensive, global health strategy. Because in the twenty-first century, we are called to act by our conscience and our common interest. When a child dies of a preventable illness in Accra, that diminishes us everywhere. And when disease goes unchecked in any corner of the world, we know that it can spread across oceans and continents.

That is why my Administration has committed $63 billion to meet these challenges. Building on the strong efforts of President Bush, we will carry forward the fight against HIV/AIDS. We will pursue the goal of ending deaths from malaria and tuberculosis, and eradicating polio. We will fight neglected tropical disease. And we won't confront illnesses in isolation—we will invest in public health systems that promote wellness, and focus on the health of mothers and children.

As we partner on behalf of a healthier future, we must also stop the destruction that comes not from illness, but from human beings—and so the final area that I will address is conflict.

Now let me be clear: Africa is not the crude caricature of a continent at war. But for far too many Africans, conflict is a part of life, as constant as the sun. There are wars over land and wars over resources. And it is still far too easy for those without conscience to manipulate whole communities into fighting among faiths and tribes.

These conflicts are a millstone around Africa's neck. We all have many identities—of tribe and ethnicity; of religion and nationality. But defining oneself in opposition to someone who belongs to a different tribe, or who worships a different prophet, has no place in the twenty-first century. Africa's diversity should be a source of strength, not a cause for division. We are all God's children. We all share common aspirations—to live in peace and security; to access education and opportunity; to love our families, our communities, and our faith. That is our common humanity.

That is why we must stand up to inhumanity in our midst. It is never justifiable to target innocents in the name of ideology. It is the death sentence of a society to force children to kill in wars. It is the ultimate mark of criminality and cowardice to condemn women to relentless and systematic rape. We must bear witness to the value of every child in Darfur and the dignity of every woman in Congo. No faith or culture should condone the outrages against them. All of us must strive for the peace and security necessary for progress.

Africans are standing up for this future. Here, too, Ghana is helping to point the way forward. Ghanaians should take pride in your contributions to peacekeeping from Congo to Liberia to Lebanon, and in your efforts to resist the scourge of the drug trade. We welcome the steps that are being taken by organizations like the African Union and ECOWAS to better resolve conflicts, keep the peace, and support those in need. And we encourage the vision of a strong, regional security architecture that can bring effective, transnational force to bear when needed.

America has a responsibility to advance this vision, not just with words, but with support that strengthens African capacity. When there is genocide in Darfur or terrorists in

Somalia, these are not simply African problems—they are global security challenges, and they demand a global response. That is why we stand ready to partner through diplomacy, technical assistance, and logistical support, and will stand behind efforts to hold war criminals accountable. And let me be clear: our Africa Command is focused not on establishing a foothold in the continent, but on confronting these common challenges to advance the security of America, Africa and the world.

In Moscow, I spoke of the need for an international system where the universal rights of human beings are respected, and violations of those rights are opposed. That must include a commitment to support those who resolve conflicts peacefully, to sanction and stop those who don't, and to help those who have suffered. But ultimately, it will be vibrant democracies like Botswana and Ghana which roll back the causes of conflict, and advance the frontiers of peace and prosperity.

As I said earlier, Africa's future is up to Africans.

The people of Africa are ready to claim that future. In my country, African-Americans—including so many recent immigrants—have thrived in every sector of society. We have done so despite a difficult past, and we have drawn strength from our African heritage. With strong institutions and a strong will, I know that Africans can live their dreams in Nairobi and Lagos; in Kigali and Kinshasa; in Harare and right here in Accra.

Fifty-two years ago, the eyes of the world were on Ghana. And a young preacher named Martin Luther King traveled here, to Accra, to watch the Union Jack come down and the Ghanaian flag go up. This was before the march on Washington or the success of the civil rights movement in my country. Dr. King was asked how he felt while watching the birth of a nation. And he said: "It renews my conviction in the ultimate triumph of justice."

Now, that triumph must be won once more, and it must be won by you. And I am particularly speaking to the young people. In places like Ghana, you make up over half of the population. Here is what you must know: the world will be what you make of it.

You have the power to hold your leaders accountable, and to build institutions that serve the people. You can serve in your communities, and harness your energy and education to create new wealth and build new connections to the world. You can conquer disease, end conflicts, and make change from the bottom up. You can do that. Yes you can. Because in this moment, history is on the move.

But these things can only be done if you take responsibility for your future. It won't be easy. It will take time and effort. There will be suffering and setbacks. But I can promise you this: America will be with you. As a partner. As a friend. Opportunity won't come from any other place, though—it must come from the decisions that you make, the things that you do, and the hope that you hold in your hearts.

Freedom is your inheritance. Now, it is your responsibility to build upon freedom's foundation. And if you do, we will look back years from now to places like Accra and say that this was the time when the promise was realized—this was the moment when prosperity was forged; pain was overcome; and a new era of progress began. This can be the time when we witness the triumph of justice once more. Thank you.

⇥ JOINT SESSION OF CONGRESS ⇤
ON HEALTH CARE
SEPTEMBER 9, 2009

So tonight, I return to speak to all of you about an issue that is central to that future—and that is the issue of health care.

I am not the first President to take up this cause, but I am determined to be the last. [*Applause.*] It has now been nearly a century since Theodore Roosevelt first called for health care reform. And ever since, nearly every President and Congress, whether Democrat or Republican, has attempted to meet this challenge in some way. A bill for comprehensive health reform was first introduced by John Dingell Sr. in 1943. Sixty-five years later, his son continues to introduce that same bill at the beginning of each session. [*Applause.*]

Our collective failure to meet this challenge—year after year, decade after decade—has led us to the breaking point. Everyone understands the extraordinary hardships that are placed on the uninsured, who live every day just one accident or illness away from bankruptcy. These are not primarily people on welfare. These are middle-class Americans. Some can't get insurance on the job. Others are self-employed and can't afford it, since buying insurance on your own costs you three times as much as the coverage you get from your employer. Many other Americans who are willing and able to pay are still denied insurance due to previous illnesses or conditions that insurance companies decide are too risky or too expensive to cover.

We are the only democracy—the only advanced democracy on Earth—the only wealthy nation—that allows such hardship for millions of its people. There are now more than 30 million American citizens who cannot get coverage. In just a two-year period, one in every three Americans goes without health care coverage at some point. And every day, 14,000 Americans lose their coverage. In other words, it can happen to anyone.

But the problem that plagues the health care system is not just a problem for the uninsured. Those who do have insurance have never had less security and stability than they do today. More and more Americans worry that if you move, lose your job, or change your job, you'll lose your health insurance too. More and more Americans pay their premiums, only to discover that their insurance company has dropped their coverage when they get sick, or won't pay the full cost of care. It happens every day.

One man from Illinois lost his coverage in the middle of chemotherapy because his insurer found that he hadn't reported gallstones that he didn't even know about. They delayed his treatment, and he died because of it. Another woman from Texas was about to get a double mastectomy when her insurance company canceled her policy because she forgot to declare a case of acne. By the time she had her insurance reinstated, her breast cancer had more than doubled in size. That is heart-breaking, it is wrong, and no one should be treated that way in the United States of America. [*Applause.*]

Then there's the problem of rising cost. We spend one and a half times more per person on health care than any other country, but we aren't any healthier for it. This is one of the reasons that insurance premiums have gone up three times faster than wages. It's why so many employers—especially small businesses—are forcing their employees to pay more for insurance, or are dropping their coverage entirely. It's why so many aspiring entrepreneurs cannot afford to open a business in the first place, and why American businesses that compete internationally—like our automakers—are at a huge disadvantage. And it's why those of us with health insurance are also paying a hidden and growing tax for those without it—about $1,000 per year that pays for somebody else's emergency room and charitable care.

Finally, our health care system is placing an unsustainable burden on taxpayers. When health care costs grow at the rate they have, it puts greater pressure on programs like Medicare and Medicaid. If we do nothing to slow these skyrocketing costs, we will eventually be spending more on Medicare and Medicaid than every other government program combined. Put simply, our health care problem is our deficit problem. Nothing else even comes close. Nothing else. [*Applause.*]

Now, these are the facts. Nobody disputes them. We know we must reform this system. The question is how.

There are those on the left who believe that the only way to fix the system is through a single-payer system like Canada's—[*applause*]—where we would severely restrict the private insurance market and have the government provide coverage for everybody. On the right, there are those who argue that we should end employer-based systems and leave individuals to buy health insurance on their own.

I've said—I have to say that there are arguments to be made for both these approaches. But either one would represent a radical shift that would disrupt the health care most people currently have. Since health care represents one-sixth of our economy, I believe it makes more sense to build on what works and fix what doesn't, rather than try to build an entirely new system from scratch. [*Applause.*] And that is precisely what those of you in Congress have tried to do over the past several months.

During that time, we've seen Washington at its best and at its worst.

We've seen many in this chamber work tirelessly for the better part of this year to offer thoughtful ideas about how to achieve reform. Of the five committees asked to develop bills, four have completed their work, and the Senate Finance Committee announced today that it will move forward next week. That has never happened before. Our overall efforts have been supported by an unprecedented coalition of doctors and nurses; hospitals, seniors' groups, and even drug companies—many of whom opposed reform in the past. And there is agreement in this chamber on about 80 percent of what needs to be done, putting us closer to the goal of reform than we have ever been.

But what we've also seen in these last months is the same partisan spectacle that only hardens the disdain many Americans have toward their own government. Instead of honest debate, we've seen scare tactics. Some have dug into unyielding ideological camps that offer no hope of compromise. Too many have used this as an opportunity to score short-term political points, even if it robs the country of our opportunity to solve a long-term challenge. And out of this blizzard of charges and counter-charges, confusion has reigned.

Well, the time for bickering is over. The time for games has passed. [*Applause.*] Now is the season for action. Now is when we must bring the best ideas of both parties together, and show the American people that we can still do what we were sent here to do. Now is the time to deliver on health care. Now is the time to deliver on health care.

The plan I'm announcing tonight would meet three basic goals. It will provide more security and stability to those who have health insurance. It will provide insurance for those who don't. And it will slow the growth of health care costs for our families, our businesses, and our government. [*Applause.*] It's a plan that asks everyone to take responsibility for meeting this challenge—not just government, not just insurance companies, but everybody, including employers and individuals. And it's a plan that incorporates ideas from senators and congressmen, from Democrats and Republicans—and yes, from some of my opponents in both the primary and general election.

Here are the details that every American needs to know about this plan. First, if you are among the hundreds of millions of Americans who already have health insurance through your job, or Medicare, or Medicaid, or the VA, nothing in this plan will require you or your employer to change the coverage or the doctor you have. [*Applause.*] Let me repeat this: Nothing in our plan requires you to change what you have.

What this plan will do is make the insurance you have work better for you. Under this plan, it will be against the law for insurance companies to deny you coverage because of a preexisting condition. [*Applause.*] As soon as I sign this bill, it will be against the law for insurance companies to drop your coverage when you get sick or water it down when you need it the most. [*Applause.*] They will no longer be able to place some arbitrary cap on the amount of coverage you can receive in a given year or in a lifetime. [*Applause.*] We will place a limit on how much you can be charged for out-of-pocket expenses, because in the United States of America, no one should go broke because they get sick. [*Applause.*] And insurance companies will be required to cover, with no extra charge, routine checkups and preventive care, like mammograms and colonoscopies—[*applause*]—because there's no reason we shouldn't be catching diseases like breast cancer and colon cancer before they get worse. That makes sense, it saves money, and it saves lives. [*Applause.*]

Now, that's what Americans who have health insurance can expect from this plan—more security and more stability.

Now, if you're one of the tens of millions of Americans who don't currently have health insurance, the second part of this plan will finally offer you quality, affordable choices. [*Applause.*] If you lose your job or you change your job, you'll be able to get coverage. If you strike out on your own and start a small business, you'll be able to get coverage. We'll do this by creating a new insurance exchange—a marketplace where individuals and small businesses will be able to shop for health insurance at competitive prices. Insurance companies will have an incentive to participate in this exchange because it lets them compete for millions of new customers. As one big group, these customers will have greater leverage to bargain with the insurance companies for better prices and quality coverage. This is how large companies and government employees get affordable insurance. It's how everyone in this Congress gets affordable insurance. And it's time to give every American the same opportunity that we give ourselves. [*Applause.*]

Now, for those individuals and small businesses who still can't afford the lower-priced insurance available in the exchange, we'll provide tax credits, the size of which will be based on your need. And all insurance companies that want access to this new marketplace will have to abide by the consumer protections I already mentioned. This exchange will take effect in four years, which will give us time to do it right. In the meantime, for those Americans who can't get insurance today because they have preexisting medical conditions, we will immediately offer low-cost coverage that will protect you against financial ruin if you become seriously ill. [*Applause.*] This was a good idea when Senator John McCain proposed it in the campaign, it's a good idea now, and we should all embrace it. [*Applause.*]

Now, even if we provide these affordable options, there may be those—especially the young and the healthy—who still want to take the risk and go without coverage. There may still be companies that refuse to do right by their workers by giving them coverage. The problem is, such irresponsible behavior costs all the rest of us money. If there are affordable options and people still don't sign up for health insurance, it means we pay for these people's expensive emergency room visits. If some businesses don't provide workers health care, it forces the rest of us to pick up the tab when their workers get sick, and gives those businesses an unfair advantage over their competitors. And unless everybody does their part, many of the insurance reforms we seek—especially requiring insurance companies to cover preexisting conditions—just can't be achieved.

And that's why under my plan, individuals will be required to carry basic health insurance—just as most states require you to carry auto insurance. [*Applause.*] Likewise— likewise, businesses will be required to either offer their workers health care, or chip in to help cover the cost of their workers. There will be a hardship waiver for those individuals who still can't afford coverage, and 95 percent of all small businesses, because of their size and narrow profit margin, would be exempt from these requirements. [*Applause.*] But we can't have large businesses and individuals who can afford coverage game the system by avoiding responsibility to themselves or their employees. Improving our health care system only works if everybody does their part.

And while there remain some significant details to be ironed out, I believe—[*laughter*]—I believe a broad consensus exists for the aspects of the plan I just outlined: consumer protections for those with insurance, an exchange that allows individuals and small businesses to purchase affordable coverage, and a requirement that people who can afford insurance get insurance.

And I have no doubt that these reforms would greatly benefit Americans from all walks of life, as well as the economy as a whole. Still, given all the misinformation that's been spread over the past few months, I realize— [*applause*]—I realize that many Americans have grown nervous about reform. So tonight I want to address some of the key controversies that are still out there.

Some of people's concerns have grown out of bogus claims spread by those whose only agenda is to kill reform at any cost. The best example is the claim made not just by radio and cable talk show hosts, but by prominent politicians, that we plan to set up panels of bureaucrats with the power to kill off senior citizens. Now, such a charge would be laughable if it weren't so cynical and irresponsible. It is a lie, plain and simple. [*Applause.*]

There are also those who claim that our reform efforts would insure illegal immigrants. This, too, is false. The reforms—the reforms I'm proposing would not apply to those who are here illegally.

[*Representative Joe Wilson calls out, "You lie!"—boos.*]

It's not true. And one more misunderstanding I want to clear up—under our plan, no federal dollars will be used to fund abortions, and federal conscience laws will remain in place. [*Applause.*]

Now, my health care proposal has also been attacked by some who oppose reform as a "government takeover" of the entire health care system. As proof, critics point to a provision in our plan that allows the uninsured and small businesses to choose a publicly sponsored insurance option, administered by the government just like Medicaid or Medicare. [*Applause.*]

So let me set the record straight here. My guiding principle is, and always has been, that consumers do better when there is choice and competition. That's how the market works. [*Applause.*] Unfortunately, in 34 states, 75 percent of the insurance market is controlled by five or fewer companies. In Alabama, almost 90 percent is controlled by just one company. And without competition, the price of insurance goes up and quality goes down. And it makes it easier for insurance companies to treat their customers badly—by cherry-picking the healthiest individuals and trying to drop the sickest, by overcharging small businesses who have no leverage, and by jacking up rates.

Insurance executives don't do this because they're bad people; they do it because it's profitable. As one former insurance executive testified before Congress, insurance companies are not only encouraged to find reasons to drop the seriously ill, they are rewarded for it. All of this is in service of meeting what this former executive called "Wall Street's relentless profit expectations."

Now, I have no interest in putting insurance companies out of business. They provide a legitimate service, and employ a lot of our friends and neighbors. I just want to hold them accountable. [*Applause.*] And the insurance reforms that I've already mentioned would do just that. But an additional step we can take to keep insurance companies honest is by making a not-for-profit public option available in the insurance exchange. [*Applause.*] Now, let me be clear. Let me be clear. It would only be an option for those who don't have insurance. No one would be forced to choose it, and it would not impact those of you who already have insurance. In fact, based on Congressional Budget Office estimates, we believe that less than 5 percent of Americans would sign up.

Despite all this, the insurance companies and their allies don't like this idea. They argue that these private companies can't fairly compete with the government. And they'd be right if taxpayers were subsidizing this public insurance option. But they won't be. I've insisted that like any private insurance company, the public insurance option would have to be self-sufficient and rely on the premiums it collects. But by avoiding some of the overhead that gets eaten up at private companies by profits and excessive administrative costs and executive salaries, it could provide a good deal for consumers, and would also keep pressure on private insurers to keep their policies affordable and treat their customers better, the same way public colleges and universities provide additional choice and competition to students without in any way inhibiting a vibrant system of private colleges and universities. [*Applause.*]

Now, it is—it's worth noting that a strong majority of Americans still favor a public insurance option of the sort I've proposed tonight. But its impact shouldn't be exaggerated—by the left or the right or the media. It is only one part of my plan, and shouldn't be used as a handy excuse for the usual Washington ideological battles. To my progressive friends, I would remind you that for decades, the driving idea behind reform has been to end insurance company abuses and make coverage available for those without it. [*Applause.*] The public option—the public option is only a means to that end—and we should remain open to other ideas that accomplish our ultimate goal. And to my Republican friends, I say that rather than making wild claims about a government takeover of health care, we should work together to address any legitimate concerns you may have. [*Applause.*]

For example—for example, some have suggested that the public option go into effect only in those markets where insurance companies are not providing affordable policies. Others have proposed a co-op or another non-profit entity to administer the plan. These are all constructive ideas worth exploring. But I will not back down on the basic principle that if Americans can't find affordable coverage, we will provide you with a choice. [*Applause.*] And I will make sure that no government bureaucrat or insurance company bureaucrat gets between you and the care that you need. [*Applause.*]

Finally, let me discuss an issue that is a great concern to me, to members of this chamber, and to the public—and that's how we pay for this plan.

And here's what you need to know. First, I will not sign a plan that adds one dime to our deficits—either now or in the future. [*Applause.*] I will not sign it if it adds one dime to the deficit, now or in the future, period. And to prove that I'm serious, there will be a provision in this plan that requires us to come forward with more spending cuts if the savings we promised don't materialize. [*Applause.*] Now, part of the reason I faced a trillion-dollar deficit when I walked in the door of the White House is because too many initiatives over the last decade were not paid for—from the Iraq war to tax breaks for the wealthy. [*Applause.*] I will not make that same mistake with health care.

Second, we've estimated that most of this plan can be paid for by finding savings within the existing health care system, a system that is currently full of waste and abuse. Right now, too much of the hard-earned savings and tax dollars we spend on health care don't make us any healthier. That's not my judgment—it's the judgment of medical professionals across this country. And this is also true when it comes to Medicare and Medicaid.

In fact, I want to speak directly to seniors for a moment, because Medicare is another issue that's been subjected to demagoguery and distortion during the course of this debate.

More than four decades ago, this nation stood up for the principle that after a lifetime of hard work, our seniors should not be left to struggle with a pile of medical bills in their later years. That's how Medicare was born. And it remains a sacred trust that must be passed down from one generation to the next. [*Applause.*] And that is why not a dollar of the Medicare trust fund will be used to pay for this plan. [*Applause.*]

The only thing this plan would eliminate is the hundreds of billions of dollars in waste and fraud, as well as unwarranted subsidies in Medicare that go to insurance companies—subsidies that do everything to pad their profits but don't improve the care of seniors. And we will also create an independent commission of doctors and medical experts charged with identifying more waste in the years ahead. [*Applause.*]

Now, these steps will ensure that you—America's seniors—get the benefits you've been promised. They will ensure that Medicare is there for future generations. And we can use some of the savings to fill the gap in coverage that forces too many seniors to pay thousands of dollars a year out of their own pockets for prescription drugs. [*Applause.*] That's what this plan will do for you. So don't pay attention to those scary stories about how your benefits will be cut, especially since some of the same folks who are spreading these tall tales have fought against Medicare in the past and just this year supported a budget that would essentially have turned Medicare into a privatized voucher program. That will not happen on my watch. I will protect Medicare. [*Applause.*]

Now, because Medicare is such a big part of the health care system, making the program more efficient can help usher in changes in the way we deliver health care that can reduce costs for everybody. We have long known that some places—like the Intermountain Healthcare in Utah or the Geisinger Health System in rural Pennsylvania—offer high-quality care at costs below average. So the commission can help encourage the adoption of these common-sense best practices by doctors and medical professionals throughout the system—everything from reducing hospital infection rates to encouraging better coordination between teams of doctors.

Reducing the waste and inefficiency in Medicare and Medicaid will pay for most of this plan. [*Applause.*] Now, much of the rest would be paid for with revenues from the very same drug and insurance companies that stand to benefit from tens of millions of new customers. And this reform will charge insurance companies a fee for their most expensive policies, which will encourage them to provide greater value for the money—an idea which has the support of Democratic and Republican experts. And according to these same experts, this modest change could help hold down the cost of health care for all of us in the long run.

Now, finally, many in this chamber—particularly on the Republican side of the aisle—have long insisted that reforming our medical malpractice laws can help bring down the cost of health care. [*Applause.*] Now—there you go. There you go. Now, I don't believe malpractice reform is a silver bullet, but I've talked to enough doctors to know that defensive medicine may be contributing to unnecessary costs. [*Applause.*] So I'm proposing that we move forward on a range of ideas about how to put patient safety first and let doctors focus on practicing medicine. [*Applause.*] I know that the Bush administration considered authorizing demonstration projects in individual states to test these ideas. I think it's a good idea, and I'm directing my Secretary of Health and Human Services to move forward on this initiative today. [*Applause.*]

Now, add it all up, and the plan I'm proposing will cost around $900 billion over ten years—less than we have spent on the Iraq and Afghanistan wars, and less than the tax cuts for the wealthiest few Americans that Congress passed at the beginning of the previous administration. [*Applause.*] Now, most of these costs will be paid for with money already being spent—but spent badly—in the existing health care system. The plan will not add to our deficit. The middle class will realize greater security, not higher taxes. And if we are able to slow the growth of health care costs by just one-tenth of 1 percent each year—one-tenth of 1 percent—it will actually reduce the deficit by $4 trillion over the long term.

Now, this is the plan I'm proposing. It's a plan that incorporates ideas from many of the people in this room tonight—Democrats and Republicans. And I will continue to seek common ground in the weeks ahead. If you come to me with a serious set of proposals, I will be there to listen. My door is always open.

But know this: I will not waste time with those who have made the calculation that it's better politics to kill this plan than to improve it. [*Applause.*] I won't stand by while the special interests use the same old tactics to keep things exactly the way they are. If you misrepresent what's in this plan, we will call you out. [*Applause.*] And I will not—and I will not accept the status quo as a solution. Not this time. Not now.

Everyone in this room knows what will happen if we do nothing. Our deficit will grow. More families will go bankrupt. More businesses will close. More Americans will lose their coverage when they are sick and need it the most. And more will die as a result. We know these things to be true.

That is why we cannot fail. Because there are too many Americans counting on us to succeed—the ones who suffer silently, and the ones who shared their stories with us at town halls, in e-mails, and in letters.

I received one of those letters a few days ago. It was from our beloved friend and colleague, Ted Kennedy. He had written it back in May, shortly after he was told that his illness was terminal. He asked that it be delivered upon his death.

In it, he spoke about what a happy time his last months were, thanks to the love and support of family and friends, his wife, Vicki, his amazing children, who are all here tonight. And he expressed confidence that this would be the year that health care reform—"that great unfinished business of our society," he called it—would finally pass. He repeated the truth that health care is decisive for our future prosperity, but he also reminded me that "it concerns more than material things." "What we face," he wrote, "is above all a moral issue; at stake are not just the details of policy, but fundamental principles of social justice and the character of our country."

I've thought about that phrase quite a bit in recent days—the character of our country. One of the unique and wonderful things about America has always been our self-reliance, our rugged individualism, our fierce defense of freedom, and our healthy skepticism of government. And figuring out the appropriate size and role of government has always been a source of rigorous and, yes, sometimes angry debate. That's our history.

For some of Ted Kennedy's critics, his brand of liberalism represented an affront to American liberty. In their minds, his passion for universal health care was nothing more than a passion for big government.

But those of us who knew Teddy and worked with him here—people of both parties—know that what drove him was something more. His friend Orrin Hatch—he knows that. They worked together to provide children with health insurance. His friend John McCain knows that. They worked together on a Patient's Bill of Rights. His friend Chuck Grassley knows that. They worked together to provide health care to children with disabilities.

On issues like these, Ted Kennedy's passion was born not of some rigid ideology, but of his own experience. It was the experience of having two children stricken with cancer. He never forgot the sheer terror and helplessness that any parent feels when a child is badly sick. And he was able to imagine what it must be like for those without insurance, what it would be like to have to say to a wife or a child or an aging parent, there is something that could make you better, but I just can't afford it.

That large-heartedness—that concern and regard for the plight of others—is not a partisan feeling. It's not a Republican or a Democratic feeling. It, too, is part of the American character—our ability to stand in other people's shoes; a recognition that we are all in this together, and when fortune turns against one of us, others are there to lend a helping hand; a belief that in this country, hard work and responsibility should be rewarded by some measure of security and fair play; and an acknowledgment that sometimes government has to step in to help deliver on that promise.

This has always been the history of our progress. In 1935, when over half of our seniors could not support themselves and millions had seen their savings wiped away, there were those who argued that Social Security would lead to socialism, but the men and women of Congress stood fast, and we are all the better for it. In 1965, when some argued that Medicare represented a government takeover of health care, members of Congress—Democrats and Republicans—did not back down. They joined together so that all of us could enter our golden years with some basic peace of mind.

You see, our predecessors understood that government could not, and should not, solve every problem. They understood that there are instances when the gains in security from government action are not worth the added constraints on our freedom. But they also understood that the danger of too much government is matched by the perils of too little; that without the leavening hand of wise policy, markets can crash, monopolies can stifle competition, the vulnerable can be exploited. And they knew that when any government measure, no matter how carefully crafted or beneficial, is subject to scorn; when any efforts to help people in need are attacked as un-American; when facts and reason are thrown overboard and only timidity passes for wisdom, and we can no longer even engage in a civil conversation with each other over the things that truly matter—that at that point we don't merely lose our capacity to solve big challenges. We lose something essential about ourselves.

That was true then. It remains true today. I understand how difficult this health care debate has been. I know that many in this country are deeply skeptical that government is looking out for them. I understand that the politically safe move would be to kick the can further down the road—to defer reform one more year, or one more election, or one more term.

But that is not what the moment calls for. That's not what we came here to do. We did not come to fear the future. We came here to shape it. I still believe we can act even when it's hard. [*Applause.*] I still believe—I still believe that we can act when it's hard. I still believe we can replace acrimony with civility, and gridlock with progress. I still believe we can do great things, and that here and now we will meet history's test.

Because that's who we are. That is our calling. That is our character. Thank you, God bless you, and may God bless the United States of America. [*Applause.*]

ENDNOTES

INTRODUCTION

1. *The Times*, "Europe Shows Love for Barack Obama—Unfortunately It Has No Vote," June 7, 2008.

2. Such as in May 2008 at a Portland, Oregon rally.

3. Interview on ABC News, "This Week with George Stephanopoulos," August 10, 2008.

CHAPTER 2

1. Full text of Senator Barack Obama's announcement for president, Springfield, IL, February 10, 2007.

2. Remarks of Senator Barack Obama: primary night, Raleigh, NC, May 6, 2008.

3. Remarks of Senator Barack Obama: Pennsylvania Primary Night, Evansville, IN, April 22, 2008.

4. Full text of Senator Barack Obama's announcement for president, Springfield, IL, February 10, 2007.

5. Remarks of Senator Barack Obama: final primary night, St. Paul, MN, June 03, 2008.

CHAPTER 3

1. Jesse Jackson, CNN interview, July 10, 2008.

2. Remarks of Senator Barack Obama: Virginia Jefferson-Jackson dinner, Richmond, VA, February 9, 2008.

3. CNN Interview immediately following the keynote address.

4. *New York Times*, "As Quickly as Overnight, a Democratic Star is Born," March 18, 2004

5. *New York Times*, "The democrats; The convention in Boston—The Illinois candidate; Day After, Keynote Speaker Finds Admirers Everywhere," July 29, 2004.

6. Remarks of Senator Barack Obama: Kennedy endorsement event, Washington, DC, January 28, 2008.

7. Reported in *New York Times*, "As Quickly as Overnight, a Democratic Star Is Born," March 18, 2004.

8. Remarks of Senator Barack Obama: AP annual luncheon, Washington, DC, April 14, 2008.

9. Remarks of Senator Barack Obama: primary night, Raleigh, NC, May 6, 2008.

10. CNN, June 3, 2008.

11. Remarks of Senator Barack Obama: "A More Perfect Union," Philadelphia, PA, March 18, 2008.

12. Remarks of Senator Barack Obama: Kennedy endorsement event, Washington, DC, January 28, 2008.

13. Remarks of Senator Barack Obama: Kennedy endorsement event, Washington, DC, January 28, 2008.

14. Remarks of Senator Barack Obama: discussion with working women, Albuquerque, NM, June 23, 2008.

15. Remarks of Senator Barack Obama: A Metropolitan Strategy for America's Future, Miami, FL, June 21, 2008.

16. Keynote Address at the 2004 Democratic National Convention, July 27, 2004.

17. Remarks of Senator Barack Obama: "A More Perfect Union," Philadelphia, PA, March 18, 2008.

18. Remarks of Senator Barack Obama: The Great Need of the Hour, Atlanta, GA, January 20, 2008.

19. Remarks of Senator Barack Obama: Remembering Dr. Martin Luther King, Jr., Fort Wayne, IN, April 04, 2008.

CHAPTER 4

1. Remarks of Senator Barack Obama: Our Moment Is Now, Des Moines, IA, December 27, 2007.

2. Remarks of Senator Barack Obama: South Carolina victory speech, Columbia, SC, January 26, 2008.

3. Remarks of Senator Barack Obama: Our Moment Is Now, Des Moines, IA, December 27, 2007.

4. Remarks of Senator Barack Obama: Our Kids, Our Future, Manchester, NH, November 20, 2007.

5. Remarks of Senator Barack Obama: A Call to Serve, Mt. Vernon, IA, December 5, 2007.

6. Remarks of Senator Barack Obama: final primary night, St. Paul, MN, June 3, 2008.

7. Remarks of Senator Barack Obama: Our Moment Is Now, Des Moines, IA, December 27, 2007.

CHAPTER 5

1. *Houston Chronicle.*

2. Remarks by Barack Obama at the Robert F. Kennedy Human Rights Award Ceremony, November 16, 2005.

3. Remarks by Barack Obama: final primary night, St. Paul, MN, June 3, 2008.

4. Remarks of Senator Barack Obama: Iowa Caucus Night, Des Moines, IA , January 3, 2008.

5. Remarks by Barack Obama: Kennedy endorsement event, Washington, DC, January 28, 2008.

6. Also known as fictio.

7. Keynote address at the 2004 Democratic National Convention, July 27, 2004.

8. Remarks by Barack Obama: Iowa caucus night, Des Moines, IA , January 3, 2008,

9. Remarks by Barack Obama: The Great Need of the Hour, Atlanta, GA, January 20, 2008.

10. Remarks by Barack Obama: A More Perfect Union, Philadelphia, PA, March 18, 2008.

11. Remarks by Barack Obama: Our Kids, Our Future, Manchester, NH, November 20, 2007.

12. Remarks by Barack Obama: Our Kids, Our Future, Manchester, NH, November 20, 2007.

13. Remarks by Barack Obama: Our Kids, Our Future, Manchester, NH, November 20, 200.

CHAPTER 6

1. Remarks of Barack Obama: final primary night, St. Paul, MN, June 3, 2008.

2. Remarks of Barack Obama: Virginia Jefferson-Jackson dinner, Richmond, VA, February 9, 2008.

3. Barack Obama's announcement for president, Springfield, IL, February 10, 2007.

4. Remarks of Barack Obama: Iowa caucus night, Des Moines, IA , January 3, 2008.

5. Remarks of Barack Obama: Our Moment Is Now, Des Moines, IA, December 27, 2007.

6. Remarks of Barack Obama: Our Moment Is Now, Des Moines, IA, December 27, 2007.

7. Remarks of Barack Obama: New Hampshire Primary, Nashua, NH, January 8, 2008.

8. Remarks of Barack Obama: South Carolina victory speech, Columbia, SC, January 26, 2008.

CHAPTER 7

1. Remarks by Barack Obama: Our Moment Is Now, Des Moines, IA, December 27, 2007.

2. Remarks by Barack Obama: Virginia Jefferson-Jackson Dinner, Richmond, VA, February 9, 2008.

3. Remarks by Barack Obama: Pennsylvania primary night, Evansville, IN, April 22, 2008.

4. Remarks by Senator Barack Obama: final primary night, St. Paul, MN, June 3, 2008.

5. Remarks of Senator Barack Obama: The Great Need of the Hour, Atlanta, GA, January 20, 2008

CHAPTER 8

1. Remarks of Barack Obama: AP annual luncheon, Washington, DC, April 14, 2008.

CHAPTER 9

1. Remarks by Barack Obama: primary night, Raleigh, NC, May 6, 2008.

2. Remarks by Barack Obama: A Call to Serve, Mt. Vernon, IA, December 5, 2007.

3. Remarks by Barack Obama: Our Moment Is Now, Des Moines, IA, December 27, 2007.

4. Ibid.

5. Remarks by Barack Obama: Virginia Jefferson-Jackson Dinner, Richmond, VA, February 9, 2008.

6. Remarks by Barack Obama: New Hampshire primary, Nashua, NH, January 8, 2008.

7. Remarks by Barack Obama: The Great Need of the Hour, Atlanta, GA, January 20, 2008.

8. Remarks by Barack Obama: final primary night, St. Paul, MN, June 3, 2008.

9. Remarks by Barack Obama: New Hampshire primary, Nashua, NH, January 8, 2008.

10. Barack Obama's announcement for president, Springfield, IL, February 10, 2007.

11. Remarks by Barack Obama: Our Moment Is Now, Des Moines, IA, December 27, 2007.